In *Take Courage, Dear Heart*, Sheena wades us into deep waters of self-reflection—holding our hand as she guides us through her witty stories and personal discoveries, each drawing us deeper into what it's like to have courage in every season of faith. Out of the water, we find ourselves challenged in our individual walks with Christ, yet blissfully drenched in relatability.

—Ashley Luciano, writer

Take Courage, Dear Heart

Take Courage, Dear Heart

God's Invitation to Know Him More Powerfully and Intimately through Our Deepest Fears

Sheena Heinrichs

Take Courage, Dear Heart
Copyright© 2024 by Sheena Heinrichs

Library of Congress Cataloging-in-Publication Data

LCCN: 2024901427 ISBN: 978-1-961732-15-5 (ebook) | ISBN: 978-1-961732-16-2 (paperback) | ISBN: 978-1-961732-17-9 (hardcover)

Scripture quotations marked ESV are taken from the ESV® Bible (The Holy Bible, English Standard Version®), copyright © 2001 by Crossway, a publishing ministry of Good News Publishers. Used by permission. All rights reserved. The ESV text may not be quoted in any publication made available to the public by a Creative Commons license. The ESV may not be translated in whole or in part into any other language.

Any internet addresses (website, blogs, etc.) and telephone numbers in this book are offered as a resource. They are not intended in any way to be or imply an endorsement from Called Creatives Publishing, nor does Called Creatives Publishing vouch for the content of these sites and numbers for the life of this book.

All rights reserved. No portion of this book may be reproduced or shared in any form – electronic, printed, photocopied, recording, or by any information storage or retrieval system, without prior written permission from the author. The use of short quotations is permitted.

Published in association with Called Creatives Publishing, www.calledcreativespublishing.com

Cover design: Called Creatives Publishing
Interior design: Sheena Heinrichs

2024 – First Edition

Table of Contents

Introduction	1
Chapter One - The Beginning	7
Chapter Two - Courage to Wait in Grief	19
Chapter Three - Courage to Pray the Most Important Prayer	31
Chapter Four - Courage to Lament	41
Chapter Five - Courage to Raise a Prodigal	53
Chapter Six - Courage to Trust	63
Chapter Seven - Courage to Release Resentment	71
Chapter Eight - Courage to Be Humble	85
Chapter Nine - Courage to Receive Love	99
Chapter Ten - Courage to Follow the Captain (or Courage to be Steadfast)	111
Appendix - Book Study Questions	123
Acknowledgments	129

Dedication

For Julia

My first writing partner, you encouraged me and pushed me to do this. I love you and I miss you.

"For I am sure that neither death nor life, nor angels nor rulers, nor things present nor things to come, nor powers, nor height nor depth, nor anything else in all creation, will be able to separate us from the love of God in Christ Jesus our Lord."

—Romans 8:38-39

Introduction

True courage is one of the most honored character traits in humanity, across all cultures, and throughout history. "You will never do anything in this world without courage. It is the greatest quality of the mind next to honor."[1] And C.S. Lewis states, "Courage is not simply one of the virtues, but the form of every virtue at the testing point."[2] Stories of courage, true or fiction, draw us in and make us feel a wee bit braver ourselves. But for me, courage has been elusive. Particularly biblical courage. For most of my Christian life, I tended to ignore the noble virtue, and then, once I did give it some attention, I found it mysterious and intangible.

The Defender, Fortress, Warrior God, who can rout our enemies with a word, or a breath, calls us to be courageous. Why? The faithful and fearsome God who calls us by name, who could march leagues ahead of us to vanquish our foes, commands us to show up to the battle. For what?

---

1 Aristotle Quotes. BrainyQuote.com, BrainyMedia Inc, 2023. https://www.brainyquote.com/quotes/aristotle_117889, accessed December 11, 2023.
2 Lewis, C. S. *The Screwtape Letters*. New York, NY: Bantam Books, 1995.

There have been several gut-wrenching seasons or circumstances in my life where, more than anything, I wanted to be put into a coma until the storm passed. I was deeply confused by the mystery of Providence. I had a measure of faith and belief in the power of God but didn't understand why I was also, weak as I am, required to engage in the fight. As Daffy Duck has said, "I'm not like other people. I don't like pain. It hurts me." (insert lisp) Whether it was watching my parents go through a divorce, experiencing the death of loved ones, having a child deal with chronic pain, or surviving periods with not enough income, I didn't want to have to face the "enemies."

Try as I might to convince God to wake me up when it is all over, this is not the primary way He calls His people to show up throughout the Bible. Many times, in the Old Testament, Israel faced an army of enemies. Each time He promises their victory, He still requires a level of action from them. At times, it is just, literally, to show up to "see the salvation of the Lord." This fact struck a chord with me several years ago, and I have been leaning hard into it ever since. What is the purpose?

The primary reason for our existence is to know God and bring Him glory, which can most fully be done when we are cognizant of His glorious power. This was something I could wrap my head around, but I found myself often arguing with God, promising that I would still give Him all the glory if He would tidy up the mess while I cowered in the corner. The truth I came to, finally, was twofold.

Our inability to glorify and worship God rather than ourselves is so much a part of our sinful nature that we desperately need a deepening awareness of God's power

Introduction

working in our lives and the world so that we can give Him the honor He so fully deserves. Secondly, His love for us is so profound that He wants us to experience complete transformation through the sanctifying power of facing trials with courage. And with Him.

As a New Testament believer, the true enemies of our faith are on physical. While I do believe that it is possible to fight a 'Just War,' there is no longer a call for the Christian to 'Holy War.' "For we do not wrestle against flesh and blood, but against the rulers, against the authorities, against the cosmic powers over this present darkness, against the spiritual forces of evil in the heavenly places." Romans 6:12. However, the circumstances we will face can still leave us terrified, with knees knocking. To stand up to them and see victory in our lives, we will have to summon courage repeatedly.

I deeply love the Chronicles of Narnia. They are some of the few books I have worn out and had to replace. My favorite moment from the entire series is from *Voyage of the Dawn Treader*. Along with Edmund, Eustace, and Lucy, the crew has been traveling by sea aboard the Dawn Treader with King Caspian. They are touring the Lone Islands and finally making their way to the last one; the island where dreams come true that lies in perpetual darkness.

At first, they are attracted to the promise of dreams coming to life until they are warned by a long-time inhabitant that it is not your daytime fantasies that will come to fruition but your *dreams;* the bizarre, confusing, and often ghastly images that come to us when we are sleeping. Suddenly, the crew is thrown into panic. Shrieks and howls ensue as their worst nightmares are playing out before them. Did I mention they were in the dark?

Take Courage, Dear Heart

Just when everything is at its worst, Lucy, sitting up in the mast, "leant her head on the edge of the fighting-top and whispered, 'Aslan, Aslan, if you ever loved us at all, send us help now.' The darkness did not grow any less, but she began to feel a little- a very, very little- better."[3]

Presently, the crew noticed something flying toward them. Gradually, they saw that it was a gloriously enormous albatross. It circled the mast three times, perched on the prow, and called out in a "strong sweet voice." Although the crew could not understand the albatross, they felt certain it could be trusted to guide them out of the darkness. The captain steered them toward the albatross and approached the light. But the part that gets me every time? The part that puts tears in my eyes even now as I write? Only Lucy heard the words the albatross spoke as it flew by, in Aslan's warm and powerful voice, "Courage, dear heart."[4]

While C.S. Lewis is not taking this word for word from scripture, I believe the sentiment speaks to a multitude of verses in the Old and New Testaments. The beautiful mixture of summoning the warrior in us to stand strong while remembering who we are, His precious children who will likely be quivering with fear at the same time.

The most powerful antidote to fear and anxiety is warrior-like courage that comes from knowing who our God is and continually showing up to watch Him work. Ultimately, all the work, all the heavy lifting is His. But He wants to build our faith and make us beautifully bold, so He compels us to summon courage.

---

3 Lewis, C. S., and Pauline Baynes. *The Voyage of the Dawn Treader: The Chronicles of Narnia*. New York, NY: HarperFestival, 2010.

4 Lewis, C. S., and Pauline Baynes. *The Voyage of the Dawn Treader: The Chronicles of Narnia*. New York, NY: HarperFestival, 2010.

Introduction

As I share stories from my own life where I finally began to apply courage to my circumstances, what I deeply hope you will see is that biblically epic courage is not meant to be saved for the "big stuff." We learn the practice of courage when we bravely face the little things: appointments we don't want to go to, hard conversations, or tricky finances. In my ongoing fight against anxiety, picturing myself marching into battle every time I had to face even a minor stressor was a marvelous discovery.

As we take tremulous steps into the unknown battlefields of sorrow, disappointment, pain, and broken dreams, the Christian knows that the sovereign God could have blazed ahead and stopped them all, but He doesn't. Instead, He does something infinitely more beautiful. He whispers, "Courage, dear heart," into the darkness, and as we move into battle, He prepares to change us in ways that never could have been possible if we had been cowards hiding under our beds.

Ultimately, a call to biblical courage is for each of us every day.

Chapter One

The Beginning

*"Accolades and happy days
They don't ever last
Stories of courage clouded up with fear"*
The Avett Brothers - *Victory*

On September 30, 2015, my father died suddenly. In the first week after his death, while trying to manage the waves of deep grief, we also discovered that he had died without a legal will, which made a complicated grief a whole lot more convoluted. This meant lawyer visits and long conversations with family members that had tense undertones, where relationships were already brittle.

His death also meant that we would need to take over the care of my aunt, who was mentally disabled and mentally ill. Along with a mental impairment, she was also a survivor of every level of abuse. As an inmate in Woodlands, a notoriously evil mental institution, in her teens, she was sexually and physically abused, all of this after being mentally abused by her parents. Logically, in her older age, Auntie Bev lashed out like a wounded animal at any effort to provide care due to a severe lack of trust. She needed so much support but wanted none. She longed for attention but bristled when it was given. Since I had already been somewhat involved with her care, I took over that role, which I was completely unqualified for. I was in over my head and terrified.

How do I describe my elderly Auntie Bev? I will start by saying that whatever image you conjure up of a little old lady, you need to abandon it. While she did have a slight hunch to her back and shuffled along, she also had bright pink streaks in her silver hair, wore skinny jeans with high-heeled sneakers, and had an affinity for faux fur. She lugged around an enormous purse filled with who-knows-what and studded it with pins she had collected for decades. Aside from the few steak dinners she bought herself when she got her pension check each month, Auntie Bev survived on cigarettes, black coffee, and processed meat. She was classified as mentally disabled but not enough to receive the required support services. Essentially, if she were not living in an apartment that my father legally owned, she would have been homeless.

A petite, wildly dressed, stooped woman of seventy-six does not sound terrifying. But she had been raised on cruel words, had spent a stint in a mental institution, and had survived for a decade on her own after running away from the mental institution. This meant that she had absolutely no filter for the nasty rants that inevitably ensued when help was offered or suggestions made. She was unpredictable, often confused, and fiercely independent.

Whenever I arrived at her apartment, Auntie Bev could possibly be happy that I'd come and ask me to take her to her favorite coffee shop where she would invariably make loud and uncharitable comments about one of the regulars

The Beginning

across the cafe. Or she might open the door with shock and disappointment that I had arrived and begin a tirade about how she didn't need any help and that I better not try to clean her apartment again. I would leave drained, bemoaning the wasted trip.

Each trip meant that I was leaving my own busy and full life with my family to venture into the unknown, erratic, and messy world of Auntie Bev. I was embarrassed when she yelled at the coffee shop waitress for getting her order slightly wrong. I would recoil at the smell of her apartment. She tried to tidy periodically but had a layer of grime that was demoralizing to be around, let alone leave another human being alone to live there. Why wouldn't she just let me clean? Why wouldn't she let me help her in the ways that I wanted to help her?

Occasionally, I was able to stand my ground and assert my will over her. When I discovered, to her horror and mine (for different reasons), that she was sleeping on an old mattress without sheets, I ignored her railings and insisted that my husband and I would bring her a new mattress and sheets. I took advantage of the momentum and declared that I would also change the sheets regularly. That day just ended in us scowling at each other.

Several months after my dad's passing, I was making the fifteen-minute drive to Auntie Bev's apartment to check in. It was a drive that I knew like the back of my hand. But when you're overwhelmed with fear, grief, doubt, and uncertainty, the back of your hand means nothing, and the familiar starts to blur. I was completely dreading my aunt's apartment and what might be waiting for me.

At one point in the drive, the highway splits; one leading me straight to her part of town and the other up and over an overpass that led to a bridge that would send me miles and at least 20 minutes out of my way. Yes, that was the lane I found myself in. I, the strong, lucid, capable one, didn't even notice what I had done until I was halfway over the bridge. I was suddenly jarred back to reality and the realization that what I was facing was too big for me: panicked breath and the prick of tears. I was afraid.

I exited the highway and rerouted myself. As I headed back over the bridge, a very surprising image popped into my head. At this point, it is rather crucial that you have a working knowledge of the Lord of the Rings movies. Of all the scripture the Holy Spirit could have used, it was the following moment that stopped me in my emotional tracks. It is when Merry is on the warhorse with Eowyn at the battle for Gondor. They are facing the bloodthirsty horde of Mordor, and their courage is flagging. They are standing stalwart with the army of Rohan, and Eowyn breathes in deeply and, with a shaky voice, says, "Courage, Merry. Courage for our friends."

The thought came out of nowhere as I crossed the Queensborough bridge over six years ago, and, like Eowyn, I took a deep breath, nodded to myself, and decided to summon courage. The fact that I am likening a visit to my aunt's wretched apartment to battling orcs is a bit overstated. But in the moment, all I sensed was God telling me that He was validating my fear by telling me I would need great courage to navigate the coming season I was heading into.

As the days and months trudged along after that moment on the bridge, I had to do more summoning and self-talk than I could have imagined. I dug into the Bible and began

The Beginning

to highlight the verses on courage. I read and reread the epic stories where He called His people to show up to battles, sometimes with little more than torches and clay jugs. Sometimes, He just called them to show up and watch Him completely win the battle. But they still had to show up. And they had to have courage.

Much like the Hero's Journey created by the original fantasy writer, Joseph Campbell, outlines, we are designed to leave the comfort of "home" and go on an adventure where we meet and vanquish foes, experience a type of death to self, and return with skills and changes in character we would never have achieved if we had shrunk back and neglected to answer the "call to action" as described in Campbell's brilliant monomyth.[5] This famous cycle has been applied to countless classic tales from Lord of the Rings to Star Wars to Harry Potter, but it is important to remember that, long before, it was perfected in the Bible.

For example, let us look at the story of Abraham and God's call for Abraham to take his son, Isaac, to the land of Moriah to sacrifice him on the altar as a burnt offering. Nowhere in the story do we see an explicit call for courage, but parent or not, I think we can confidently conclude that for Abraham to obey this shocking command, he would have had to exercise tremendous courage. While I have often heard Abraham's great faith expounded on in the teachings of this story, I have never heard about the courage Abraham, surely, had to muster, nor meditated on the beautiful God that Abraham had come to know by this point in the narrative.

---

5 Campbell, Joseph, and Cousineau Phil (ed.and Auth.). *The Hero's Journey*. San Francisco, CA: Harper and Row, 1990.

By the time Abraham is called to do the unthinkable regarding Isaac, let's look at some of the aspects of God that Abraham has witnessed. He knows that his God is a God who calls his children by name (Genesis 12:1-3). He is a God who is committed to truth and mercy (Genesis 12:10-20). He is a God who provides (Genesis 13:2). He is a God who blesses (Genesis 14:17). He is a God who makes a covenant with His people (Genesis 15). He is a God who listens to the afflicted (Genesis 16:11-15). He is a God of promise (17:15-16). He is a God who is holy and to be feared (Genesis 19:23-27). He is a God who keeps His promises (Genesis 21:1-7). He is a God who protects the vulnerable (Genesis 21:12-14).

I believe we do ourselves and others a grave disservice when we talk about the faith and courage of Abraham in this moment of obedience with Isaac without acknowledging the glorious relationship that has been developed between the Lord and Abraham over many years. At this crucial, tension-filled moment, Hebrews tells us that Abraham "considered that God was able even to raise him from the dead, from which, figuratively speaking, he did receive him back." (Hebrews 11:17-19)

A call to courageous obedience is not the cruel joke of a puppet master making us perform ridiculous tasks. It is the voice of a kind, omnipotent, faithful Father who wants us to partake in the best He has planned for us, not the worst. He wants us to know what it feels like to be terrified but still have courage coursing through us as we walk with Him into unchartered territory and watch Him provide exactly what we need. Just as He provided Abraham the ram for the sacrifice at the appropriate moment, He will provide what we need. More than that, He provides Himself and we will discover He

The Beginning

is the personification of courage. Christ, the great High Priest who has gone before us in all things, summoned the greatest courage of all in His journey to the cross.

Yes, courage is an act of faith but is not a blind faith in an unknowable God. It is a response to a God that we know and love because He has first set His love upon us and proven His own fierce courage in His salvation for us in Christ. I love this passage in Isaiah: "Behold, God is my salvation; I will trust, and will not be afraid; for the Lord God is my strength and my song and has become my salvation." (Isaiah 12:2)

When God calls us to be courageous, He is acknowledging our fear, showing us our humanity, and vindicating His grace in us. Psalm 103:13-14 says, "As a father shows compassion to his children, so the Lord shows compassion to those who fear Him. For he knows our frame; He remembers that we are dust." When our God is calling us to courage He is not saying "suck it up" as if He doesn't understand and know us. At that moment on the bridge, I felt that, in His call to courage, God was letting me know that He completely saw my fear and understood that it required more than gritted teeth and steely determination for me to navigate the coming season of my life.

"Be courageous" is God telling us that He knows it's scary. He knows it's hard, but He wants us to do it anyway. He believes we can do it because He will be with us. The call to courage and God's promise to be with us in the battle are intrinsically linked. "Have I not commanded you? Be strong and courageous. Do not be frightened and do not be dismayed, for the Lord your God is with you wherever you go." (Joshua 1:9) I believe having courage is more than an act of faith in the Triune God through the work of Christ. I believe the ability to exercise courage is in direct proportion to who you believe God to be and who you believe yourself to be in His eyes. Having an accurate perspective and knowledge, at both the head *and* the heart level, of God's character is crucial to maintaining a posture of courage.

Auntie Bev died in November of 2017, just over two years after my dad passed away. Of course, at the time, I was heartbroken. This was the end of the living relations on my dad's side. This was the last connection with him gone. But more than that, I had grown to love her. As I reflect on that time, I can rejoice in the firm and unwavering knowledge that God changed both Auntie Bev and me. While it would have been far easier to avoid the hurt and awkwardness and, sometimes, repulsion that came from caring for her, it is abundantly clear that by accepting the Lord's invitation for me to step out in courage, I was changed in beautiful ways that would not have been possible if I had run for cover.

The first gift the Lord gave me was that He started to open my eyes to Auntie Bev's beauty. She could be in the middle of a rant while traipsing down the sidewalk and if she saw a mom pushing a baby in a stroller, she would stop to say hello in a tender voice and say to me, "Sheena, look at this baby! She's so cute! She looks like your kids when they were small. Aww." Or she would talk kindly to a teenager who was living on the street, covered in tattoos and piercings. She would ask, "Did it hurt when you got that earring on your lip? I like your blue hair. See, I have pink." The teens would noticeably soften, relieved that, at least to someone, they were not invisible.

In fact, what I noticed was that it was the weak, vulnerable, and marginalized that she spoke to with kindness. Auntie

The Beginning

Bev's prickly demeanor was reserved for the proud and condescending. People like me.

To my shame, when Auntie Bev would interact with people in public at all, my initial response was embarrassment. Oddly, anyone, including a fast-food server, with a uniform caused her to feel threatened and if she bawled out the server for giving her the wrong flavor of muffin, I would share an apologetic eye roll with the affronted worker. In the beginning, when I drove her to her favorite corner store to get her cigarettes and "scratch tickets," I waited in the car so the owners of the store wouldn't know who "the niece" was. But as time passed God started to expose my snobbery. He used Auntie Bev to bring a level of humility that I am so grateful for. And in return, she experienced a level of dignity and care that she deserved.

I learned that she didn't really care what I did for her, it was the *way* I did things for her. If I showed up with a spirit of deferment, honoring the fact that she was my elder and deserving of my respect, her demeanor was much softer. When we brought in her mattress with new bedding and a fun pink quilt with matching throw pillows, I was making sure that she liked everything instead of assuming that she should be grateful. She was thrilled. Of course, it did help that my husband was with me. She preferred him. "Sheena, your husband is nicer than you." Sigh. Yes, I know.

I began to be convicted when I would get embarrassed by her and started to stand up for her whenever I had the opportunity. During her short stint in the hospital, she gave some of the nurses a hard time. Once again, it wasn't all the nurses, just the ones who talked down to her and treated her like a child. I was visiting one day when Auntie Bev got upset with a nurse for bringing her the wrong kind of juice. The nurse began to mollify her while giving me a knowing look accompanied by an eye roll.

While my aunt watched me, I met the nurse's gaze with an expression that conveyed I had no idea why she was looking at me like that and said, "My aunt asked for apple, not orange juice. If you are too busy to get it, can you tell me where I can?" Auntie Bev just looked at me with a bit of surprise that made me feel ashamed. She had deserved to know someone had her back, but until that moment, she hadn't felt that from me. I also stopped waiting in the car when she went into the corner store. I was rewarded by meeting Ali and his wife, the Iranian immigrants who honored my aunt and were thrilled to meet me; someone they had heard so much about. "Oh, hello," they beamed. "It is so nice to meet you. Your aunt is so sweet!" Humbled again.

When the time came to plan a funeral for Auntie Bev, the feelings of inadequacy came crashing down again. I am not an event planner, let alone an event for which you don't have emails or phone numbers for most people you would like to invite. But, again, the provision came. Family members offered to help with big and little details. Vivian, an older lady in Auntie Bev's building, rounded up all the other residents who knew my aunt. Even when the church called me the day before the funeral to inform me that they had double booked and we had no space available to us, another place materialized. Granted, it was the tiny community room in the dingy basement of her apartment building, but by the time we spruced it up and added photos and a table loaded with coffee and treats, it was almost inviting.

The Beginning

My family and I arrived home later that day exhausted but absolutely marveling at the way the Lord made for us. We met the sweetest people that day, and I was able to stand back and watch my husband and teenage kids interact with Iranian Ali and funny old Vivian and some rough characters from the neighborhood, all of whom truly loved my aunt.

I will be honest: in the years I was required to drive up to Auntie Bev's apartment, it never got a lot easier. Right up until the incredible day of her funeral, it required a tremendous amount of courage. But I am convinced that allowing the Lord to walk with you into unknown territory with nothing but Himself and the decision to be brave changes us in unique ways.

These experiences are a part of me, and they are a part of my family. The awe and wonder we shared on that day of her funeral was a testimony to God, showing us the level to which He was with me at each painful, awkward, frustrating, hysterical, weird, and sweet moment.

Chapter Two

Courage to Wait in Grief

*"Stories without a few let-downs are boring when told
Perfection and poems are a lie when it all unfolds."*
Judah and the Lion - *Spirit*

Before I ever encountered grief up close, I had never been told that one would require deep wells of courage to navigate the difficult and often dark terrain of death. I believe now that this is even more true when this grief includes a difficult past relationship with the person who has died. My dad's death was sudden, and the only way I can describe the ensuing season was one of complicated grief. It was confusing and often very scary. How do you grieve someone who, at certain points in your life, had been abusive? How do you reconcile the wonderful character traits of the present with the history you are still healing from?

As an adult I had, for the most part, made peace with my dad but after his death, memories of my childhood washed over me in confusion and anger. He was given to a temper and rage that often had me cowering in my bedroom or dragging my feet on my walk home from school. If I knew he would be home from work, I would have wanted to avoid being there as long as possible. From one moment to the next, I wouldn't know if he was going to call me into the kitchen to joke around and let me taste one of his beautiful culinary creations or lecture me on how I left the milk on the counter using cruel and shameful language.

But in later years, long after I had left home, he had softened, and we grew closer. He never did fully comprehend the level of hurt he had inflicted, but it was evident that he was trying so hard to change - to make amends with actions instead of words, and to treat my children, his grandchildren, with love and patience. Because of these years prior to his death, there were also times after his passing that I just flat out missed him and would feel guilty for being angry at him for the early years. Round and round it went missing, angry, guilty, repeat.

My dad was larger than life, literally and figuratively, and a storyteller that commanded a room. As a child, I would hear him begin to regale the group with a story that was so well-worn that, surely, *I won't laugh this time,* I thought. But I did. Every time. It was, in part, due to the howling response of the audience but, mostly, that he was hysterically funny. His parties were legendary, and his practical jokes were notorious; one even made the evening news. He was a Vancouver firefighter at the time and had sent out letters to several of the Schwarzenegger wanna-be's on the force.

The letter, not signed by my dad, stated that they had been chosen to be in the firemen's calendar. You know the one where they pose without shirts holding puppies or kittens. It included the address of the fake agency as well as the date. April first. He then alerted the Vancouver television news crew who were there in time to air a few of the victims before they realized they'd been played. Watching the face of the targeted firefighter transform from cocky pleasure to abject horror as the April Fools prank dawned on them was gold for my dad. He recorded the whole thing on our VHS and, to the day he died, I think that was his proudest moment.

My dad was also generous. As an adult, every time I visited, he supplied me with boxes of food: salmon that he had caught and canned, moose meat, massive cans of maple syrup. He was hospitable. Growing up, our doors were always unlocked, and our house was often full of people. There were parties where he cooked exquisite cuisine or coffee mornings with the rougher characters from the neighborhood.

Unfortunately, along with the fun and the parties and the stories and roaring laughter, could also be found a roaring rage. His own history of abuse combined with trauma from both the fire department and the navy meant that he had demons he was trying to tame with alcohol and varied distractions. Quite often, they couldn't be quelled and those closest to him bore the brunt. My mom, my brothers, and I learned to appease and avoid triggers. One of those triggers was church.

My dad hated Jesus. Well, I don't really know that. He hated Christians. That's not fair either, now that I think about it. There were a lot of individual Christians that he loved and respected. He hated organized religion. Christianity specifically. Since my mom had become a Christian shortly before they married, the tension in the home was the tightest on this point. If my mom dared defy my dad and attend church, he made life so miserable for her that she decided it wasn't worth it. So, the only time we made it to church were the times we were staying with relatives (without my dad) or during his annual hunting trips.

Despite all this, by God's amazing grace, through the teaching of my mama and a few well-timed sermons, I confessed my sin and put my hope in the resurrected Christ as a 16-year-old. At this point, my mom and I decided that, regardless of the backlash, we needed to attend church regularly. And backlash we did get, rantings, lectures, silent treatments, mocking, pleadings. However, amongst those miserable moments, there were conversations wherein I could explicitly share the gospel with my dad and seek to understand him. Sounds good, right? Like those stories with happy endings?

In my deep desire to see my dad free of his hurt and anger, I prayed and continued to share my faith with him. I was fueled by the hope from stories I heard, repeatedly, where the Christian prays and prays for their unbelieving loved one, and finally, usually on their deathbed, the dear one accepts Jesus. I am not trying to sound mocking or cynical. Every conversion story is a miracle and has served to shore up my faith. However, I would hear these stories and presume that this is how it would be with my dad. Without realizing it, my hope was in the story, not the person and character of God.

On September 30, 2015, when I heard that my dad had been rushed to the hospital, I was ready to jump in my vehicle to make the 6-hour drive, only to receive a second phone call that it was too late and that he was gone. He was gone. No last conversation. No follow-up from all the hundreds of conversations we had had. No evidence of a deathbed conversion. I was devastated by the loss, but I was also bewildered. This was not how the story was supposed to go.

Courage to Wait in Grief

Nobody, not one Christian had ever stood up in public or written in a book a story that ended like this. But the Lord, I have discovered in deepening measure, is gracious and if we let Him, He will take us on a different journey. A journey where He wants to take us to deep places, real places, that causes us to find out that we are living our own epic tale with Him and not living the lives of other people's stories.

While it would still be a few months after my dad's death before I would hear God's Spirit beckoning me on that drive to my aunt's house to come alongside Him in the battle, even with cowering little knees, I can see how He was providing sermons, circumstances, and people to pave the way for the journey He was preparing me for. One of the first people He sent my way was my friend, Pam. A tiny person, Pam is fierce with fiery eyes and a sure faith. When she saw me after my dad's passing, she marched up to me, gave me a huge hug, and then looked at me intently and said with conviction, "I know your dad wasn't a Christian and I know he died suddenly so you are probably struggling with assurance of his salvation. But I want you to know that I am praying that God will give you something. Something to give you peace and comfort. I believe He will do it."

And so did I. For three years, I kept hoping. I prayed for it with many tears. I looked and waited expectantly. I had encouraging conversations with wise and loving people: my husband, my friends, and my pastor. They urged me to remember the character of my God, His justice and benevolence. It helped, but I knew that I was waiting for something else. I knew that the thing that Pam was talking about was something that would ground me in a way that none of these conversations did. There were also times when

Take Courage, Dear Heart

I tried with gritted teeth to ignore the grief and fear and confusion. But finally, and unexpectedly, which is often how God works, it came. A precious gift.

Almost three years to the day that my dad died, I was at home sick while my husband and kids were at church. I had picked up my phone with the intention of listening to a sermon but "somehow" found myself scrolling through Facebook. After several memes and vacation pics, I stumbled across this conversation that a friend had had with her young son. She had been talking to her kids about an elderly lady who had passed away. They had discussed how sad it was that she had died, leaving behind many loved ones, but also how, since she was a Christian, she now had the privilege of seeing Jesus. This is the exact conversation:

The child: "That's the only good thing about death. Actually, there are two good things. You know the other good thing? I bet she knows if the Pharaoh is in heaven."

The mom: "The Pharaoh?"

The child: "The one who fought with Moses and drowned."

The mom: "Well. You can never know for sure, but I wouldn't really expect to see him there given he died trying to kill God's people."

The child: "Yeah. But he might have repented as the water was closing in over his head. God would have forgiven him. You never know."

As the water was closing in over his head. God would have forgiven him. You. Never. Know. At that moment, it was as if mighty water was crashing over *me*, as something deep inside, a dam I had been trying to hold up, broke. I mean I absolutely and completely wept as I had never wept

Courage to Wait in Grief

before. Two truths, from the mouth of a child, kept repeating in my mind like waves: one, he might have repented at the last moment, and two, God would have forgiven him. My God, who "does not wish that any should perish, but that all should reach repentance" (2 Peter 3:9) revealed a deeper glimpse into His character and, in that special moment, opened up my understanding. I was completely spent from crying but felt a peace and comfort that I had not known for years. I can rest in the all-knowing, sovereign, and gracious hand of my loving Father. I don't know anything definitive about my dad, but I know who my God is.

I had been someone who held on for years to the words of others. The words, mistakenly, turned into a promise that I would be guaranteed a certain experience that did not come to fruition in the way I had hoped. It is the story of the exodus and the escape from the very pharaoh I referenced earlier that turned my thoughts to Moses. If anyone had a mistaken view of how the story would unravel, it was Moses.

Having been raised in Pharaoh's court, Moses knew only privilege. We are told that he was a "fine child" who likely grew up to be handsome and strong and accustomed to his own way. As a young man, he sees a Hebrew slave being treated badly. Being a Hebrew himself, it is understandable that Moses would be impassioned with a desire for justice. But in his extreme response to kill the Egyptian guard, we can see that he was bold and had a measure of courage that stemmed from confidence in his own abilities. When Pharoah learns of Moses' actions, he vows to kill Moses, which forces Moses to flee to the deserts of Midian. His first action after arriving at a well in Midian? He stands up boldly to a group of shepherds so that some women could draw water for their flocks.

One would think that God would reward Moses for being such a champion of the oppressed, but instead, Moses is deposited as the keeper of his father-in-law's flock. For forty years he is a servant to Jethro, far from the splendors of Pharaoh's court. The biblical narrative does not let us know what Moses was thinking, but I believe it is probable that his mind would have often wandered to the thousands of Hebrews, his people, still enslaved in Egypt. What was God up to? How could they possibly ever be freed? All Moses could do was wonder and wait.

Often courage can be waiting, retreating and watching God move and act in ways that you could have never imagined. It is not the same as hiding under the covers until the hard stuff is over though. Waiting in faith with the expectation that a change needs to happen in someone's life or your own heart is scary business. It is acknowledging that you do not have the power or capability to do the thing required of you. It has become crucial for me to deeply meditate on Ephesians 3:20a: "Now to Him who is able to do far more abundantly than all that we ask or think." The NIV says "imagine" instead of "think."

I have a decent imagination and I like to spend a lot of time thinking about what God can do. But the truth is that how He could act or intervene in the circumstance that is squeezing your heart right now is completely outside your capacity to brainstorm. Because I tend to be a proactive, make-it-happen kind of person, I wasted a lot of time in deep grief trying to think and imagine my way out of it. I was asking all the questions, trying to expedite the process but in the waiting

Courage to Wait in Grief

was found true courage. Not avoiding. That is cowardly. But waiting on God.

As Moses was fleeing for his life from Pharaoh to the desert, I do not believe there was a glimmer of hope that he would ever be returning to Egypt. We, maybe a glimmer. As he was tending livestock in Midian his mind could never have conceived what God had in store for him and the entire nation of Israel. Truth, as they say, is stranger than fiction.

Going into a valley of grief, I had a lot of preconceived ideas of how I was going to navigate it and what it would look like to walk out the other side. I envisioned myself meeting someone who had a last conversation with my dad giving evidence of a late hour conversion. I did not get that. I pictured times of deep sobbing at the appointed times. Instead, tears would not come when summoned and in their place would be more anger than grief. I found myself wanting to hide away from people, which was a new phenomenon for this extra extrovert. Like Moses, I started out confident in my own human strength and wisdom but quickly came up short of the reality of my human limitations and all the ways I was aware of my ignorance.

While Moses had seen a future of power and glory, God had a very different plan for him, one that involved a deep humbling of himself and equally deep submission to God's mysterious will. He had to abandon a plan that was hatched out of human reasoning and live the courageous life of waiting. For forty years. Waiting. Again, we can only speculate about how Moses spent thousands of hours caring for Jethro's flocks. But the fact that we see a very different Moses when he meets the living God at the burning bush, gives us reason to believe that much of that solitude was spent in prayer.

After forty years the arrogant, self-sufficient Moses is quickly removing his sandals and responding to God's call to lead His people out of slavery with "who am I"? "Who am I" is the voice of the humbled. It is the voice of the one who has courageously submitted to their God.

Before my dad died, I was fairly confident about the trajectory of my story in regard to how things would end with my dad based on a romanticized view of evangelism. I had boldly done my part in sharing Jesus with my dad so, surely, I was going to see "my" conversion. But when things went sideways, I realized quickly that I am not the author of my, or anyone's, story. I was sent into emotional exile. I was in a spiritual desert where all I could do was wait. The only decision I had was whether I would wait courageously by staying close to the Lord, expectant that He would lead me. "I will lead the blind in a way that they do not know, in paths that they have not known I will guide them. I will turn the darkness before them into light, the rough places into level ground. These are the things I do, and I do not forsake them." (Isaiah 42:16)

While waiting with courage also means without demanding a particular outcome or avoiding the pain that grief would require, there were many times that I did resort to petulant demands and pain-numbing tactics. I watched a lot of crappy TV, ate too much, and often avoided prayer. But I also learned that our gracious and compassionate God takes the little bits of obedience and does wonderful things.

At that moment when I read those precious words of a child talking about Pharoah, I wasn't just crushed by the relief of seeing God's answer, that my friend, Pam, convinced me would come, but I was also overwhelmed by the generosity of God and how He acknowledged my quivering attempt at courageous waiting.

To this day I have no more understanding of how and why my dad lived and died. But since that moment on Facebook while in my sickbed, I have had a profound and inexplicable peace. I still believe that, like the parable of the persistent widow in Luke 18, we are exhorted by the Lord to continue our petitions before Him and to "not lose heart" in prayer for our loved ones but the outcome will not always be what we imagine. I have learned to be more comfortable with being brave in the face of the unknown and unexpected. I have learned to be more comfortable being brave in the face of the unknown.

Chapter Three

Courage to Pray the Most Important Prayer

"I felt alone, still feel afraid
I stumble through it anyway"
Pink - *All I Know So Far*

I can clearly remember where I was sitting in my living room in January 2016. Alone in prayer, curled up in my favorite chair, and my prayer had turned into an argument with God. I had been in the middle of praying for my husband - a specific prayer and it had been on repeat for ten years. Ten. And then suddenly God said, "stop." It was that voice that isn't an actual voice, but you know, for some inexplicable reason, it's a thought that's not your own.

He was telling me to stop praying for a new job for Vern and to start praying that Vern would, more and more, love Him with all his heart. No. I didn't want to pray for that. I wanted to continue to remind the omniscient and omnipotent God that my husband wouldn't be happy unless he had a new job. Besides, from my perspective, I was scared that if I didn't continually remind God of what would make my husband happy then He might not make it happen.

My husband, an electrician, would come home looking worn from working in big, noisy construction sites. He found it monotonous and depressing and gray. For months we had been waiting to hear from the film industry where he had applied to work in the lighting design department, less gray and way more creative.

For the next week or two after being given the new prayer mission, I felt like a toddler whose favorite toy was being pried out of their chubby hands. Part of my reasoning was that I looked up to my husband and his heart for the Lord. While all of us can love God more and more through the expansion of His Kingdom and until we get to heaven, my very limited spiritual vision ascertained that *I* needed concentrated prayer to love God with all my heart, not Vern. But eventually, I relented. Every time in the months of January and February that I began to pray for a new job for Vern, I stopped myself and prayed that my husband would love the Lord with all his heart. That was all. Gradually, it became second nature.

I had been praying this way for months before I told my husband in a sheepish voice, "you know, this might sound weird, but for whatever reason, when I was praying for you a while ago about getting a new job, I'm pretty sure God was telling me to stop and only pray that you would love Him with all your heart."

I looked at him, expecting a confused expression. Instead, he considered me for a moment and then said softly, "That is what I want. I want you to pray for that." I was deeply humbled by how I could have gotten it so wrong. How could I have spent years not seeing the deepest longing of my

Courage to Pray the Most Important Prayer

husband's heart? How could I have aimed so low in my prayers and missed the mark so drastically? I had, and often still do, felt more safe and comfortable crafting and manufacturing the solutions to everyone's problems and answers to their questions.

I had congratulated myself in the past when my persistence and savvy had gotten us opportunities: free schooling for him, housing for us, friends for our kids. Instead, this moment in January 2016 marked the long hard journey of walking closely with the Lord and courageously declaring, over and over, I don't know. I don't know what will make people happy. The job, the school, the role, the haircut, the car, the outfit. I only know this: to pray "Your Will Be Done" is scary.

While I have, many years later, become more accustomed to praying this way, it can still be hard, and that kicking, screaming toddler behavior can occasionally resurface. When one of my kids is struggling with disappointment or illness, I am tempted to plead, slightly panicked, for that physical need to be provided immediately. Not much can pierce a mother's heart more than a hurting kid. But that voiceless voice of God's Spirit is faithful to call me into the deeper, unknown territory of communion with Him wherein He puts to mind a prayer for my child that is deeper, grander, and more eternal than whatever it is that I can see outwardly. For as much as we tend to share all the physical prayer needs during a Bible study, the Bible is rarely speaking to our physical circumstances but calling us, in Christ, to transcend them.

It feels safer to say, "Can you pray for my sore back?" than to say, "Can you pray that I would stop doubting the existence of God?" But the Bible is continually challenging us, even gently beckoning us to come to Him with very real and honest prayer. When we read this passage from 2 Corinthians, we see that God is seeking to encourage us in our pursuit of the higher things, the things we can't even see but, if we are honest with ourselves, know. "So, we do not lose heart. Though our outer self is wasting away, our inner self is being renewed day by day. For this light momentary affliction is preparing for us an eternal weight of glory beyond all comparison, as we look not to the things that are seen but to the things that are unseen. For the things that are seen are transient, but the things that are unseen are eternal." 2 Cor. 4:16-18

Prayer with courage leads to much less disappointment. Proverbs 13:12 says, "Hope deferred makes the heart sick, but a desire fulfilled is a tree of life." When my low-level, immediate gratification, please-change-the-things-I-can-see prayers aren't answered in the manner I envisioned, I can become frustrated, bitter, and confused. In other words, heartsick. But when I lift my eyes to the source of life, the unseen but knowable person of Christ, and pray the best prayer possible, "let me seek You and Your Kingdom," not knowing what that could look like, I am revived and at peace.

Henri Nouwen calls these "prayers of hope like the relation of a child toward his mother. All day long, the child asks for things, but the love he has for his mother does not depend on her fulfilling these wishes. The child knows that his mother will do only what is good for him, and in spite of occasional fits and a few short-lived tantrums, if he doesn't get his way, he continues to be convinced that, in the end, his mother does only what is best for him."[6]

---

6 M., Nouwen. *With Open Hands*. Notre Dame, IN: Ave Maria Press, 2007.

Courage to Pray the Most Important Prayer

I appreciate that Nouwen also acknowledges that our gracious God also welcomes the "I can't find my car keys" kind of prayers and the "please heal my cold right now" prayers. Even the "please give my husband a new job" prayers. We are still His children, after all, who happen to be human and need assistance in those moments. These kinds of prayers can even require a different kind of courage that comes from the vulnerability of not having the strength in ourselves for the little, everyday things.

But, ultimately, the courageous prayer of hope "is not directed toward the gift, but toward the one who gives it. His prayer might still contain just as many desires. However, it is not a question of having a wish come true but of expressing an unlimited faith in the giver of all good things."[7] As we continually look to the Person, rather than the outcome of the prayer, I believe we will more naturally move into the unchartered territory of the courageous prayers that change us from the inside out.

As I so easily slip back into the 'low-level' prayers, it is vital for me to remember that I am in good company. As we watch, in the New Testament, the progression of the apostle's understanding of who Jesus really is, we see how much they desire the momentary quick fix kinds of answers from Jesus. At times, it seems that the apostles aren't really progressing at all but stuck in a continual loop of misunderstanding. While their authentic devotion to Jesus is increasing, they simply cannot entirely shift their focus from the desire they have for immediate power from a Messiah that they want to deliver them, right now, from the oppressive Roman Empire.

---

7 M., Nouwen. *With Open Hands*. Notre Dame, IN: Ave Maria Press, 2007.

They are in awe of the miracles, the healings, the calming of the storm, the walking on water. It makes sense that the impending overthrowing of Caesar must be next. That He would want to change them from the inside out does not occur to them. That they need to have the mini emperor of their hearts overthrown would require more courage than they could conceive prior to Christ's death and resurrection.

Dearest Peter, in particular, gets things continually wrong. His first response to Jesus is "depart from me, for I am a sinful man, O Lord." (Luke 5:8) He recognizes that Jesus is the Christ with power but does not see the humility of a compassionate Savior. At the Mount of Transfiguration, Peter thinks he is praising Jesus for being at the same level as Moses and Elijah but missing the point again: Jesus is God and, therefore, preeminent, ruling and reigning over all things before Moses and Elijah were even born.

Even as the crucifixion was approaching, Peter is still mystified and employing human bravery when he contradicts Jesus about His own death. The famous sting, "Get behind me, Satan!" (Matthew 16:23), with which Jesus rebukes Peter, reveals Peter's human and temporal reasoning and that the true sight of a heart filled with godly courage is one that submits to the words, warnings, and teachings of the Christ.

The culmination of all Peter's misunderstandings of the true power and purpose of the incarnation is seen at the foot washing. I cannot read or think about this radical moment in history without getting goosebumps. The Lord of all creation is kneeling before His created beings to wash their dirty feet. "No," says Peter. I imagine him saying it in a hoarse whisper. Horrified because he is both humbled to his core and, equally, horrified that Jesus, the one clearly meant to destroy the

Courage to Pray the Most Important Prayer

Romans, is here to break apart and rebuild his heart rather than the material world he is trying to survive.

Jesus reminds Peter that this is it. This is the call to courage that must be answered. Jesus, at the door of your heart, wanting to come in and commune with you. Wanting to revolutionize your world at the heart level. Wanting to banish the idols, the temptations, the misplaced desires, the competing loves so that any other prayer request becomes inconsequential. Again, Peter overshoots the target, and in an attempt at human bravery, which can often take the form of legalism, he counters with his own version of Jesus' offer. "Lord, not my feet only but also my hands and my head!" (John 13: 9) No Peter, the true courage is in the quiet submission to Christ as He pursues us as His beloved, on His terms. The courage that He calls us to in prayer is, again, an invitation to show up to watch as He reforms the landscape of our inner being.

True and transformative prayer is not a simple and safe practice reserved only for polite platitudes in Bible studies. If there is any doubt of that, one only needs to read the accounts of the Garden of Gethsemane prayer of Christ. This pivotal moment is mentioned in all four gospels, but in Matthew, Mark, and Luke, it is described in grim detail with words like sorrowful, greatly distressed, troubled, agony, sweat-like drops of blood.

The most epic battle was being fought at this moment, and the incredible courage of Christ is on display through anguished prayer. Finally, on His face, Jesus proclaims the words, "My Father, if it be possible, let this cup pass from me; nevertheless, not as I will, but as you will." (Matthew 26:39) This pilgrimage prayer brought Christ to the very heart of

God and revealed to us that we are not alone in our hard prayers and that the reward may not be glory but something better; the goodness of God.

In a sermon from Tyler Staton stated that we are always seeking the glory of God, but He is wanting to give us His goodness.[8] He gave the example of Moses in Exodus 33 who, after seeing wonders untold of God's glory, is asking to see even more. But the answer from God in verse 19 is, "I will make all my goodness pass before you and will proclaim before you my name 'The Lord'." We want the power of visible answers to material questions. The miracles and the manifest presence of God. But our gracious and compassionate God is proclaiming His tender love over us as He seeks to give us Himself.

The pattern all throughout the Bible is a God whose priority is to radically change the hearts of His people. That is the Kingdom Come. In his sermon, Tyler asks, "What if I'm a person that He loves enough to trade kingdom efficiency (the outward power and glory of building God's kingdom) any day of the week for one more square inch of your heart."[9] My heart. My husband's heart. My children's hearts. Your heart. That is what He is after. That is where His kingdom was meant to reside.

Until the moment in my living room years ago, I never would have thought that there were times when one required courage to pray. Although I had been a Christian for decades, I had not realized that abandoning myself completely to God's plan for me and those I loved is abjectly terrifying. The glories,

---

8 Staton, Tyler. 2022. "Life of the Beloved". Portland, Oregon, June 26, 2022.
9 Staton, Tyler. 2022. "Life of the Beloved". Portland, Oregon, June 26, 2022.

Courage to Pray the Most Important Prayer

large and small, that I am seeking for myself and my loved ones seem like things that will make us happy and content. Therefore, it takes everything I have to shift gears and look for His goodness. His presence. His love was revealed to me on His terms.

Surprisingly, after a few months of praying in this vein, at the beginning of 2016, Vern did get the job. However, I can tell you emphatically that this is not a prayer formula for success, and there is still a large part of me that is embarrassed to admit how difficult and scary it still is to shift from praying for an outward physical need or desire to a strictly inner spiritual need. I do not believe God rewards us with the things we secretly want when we finally get our act together and figure out the way to ask for it. That is not His generous Father's heart. I believe He was going to provide Vern with the job he had wanted, but His gracious call to me months before was to begin to cultivate the courage to pray for myself and others in a way that would yield abundantly more fruit than the prayers I was more typically asking.

Sometime in the past year, I sat down in the quiet morning to eat my breakfast. As my eyes glanced around the dining room, they stopped in their tracks by the little chalkboard in the corner of the room. For years I had been writing Bible verses on the board with fancy chalk lettering. You know, as all the kitschy coffee shops and Christian moms do. But there was a new verse up there in simple, plain printing. My husband's printing: "I believe that I shall look upon the goodness of the Lord in the land of the living! Wait for the Lord! Be strong and let your heart take courage. Wait for the Lord!" (Psalm 27:13,14)

Take Courage, Dear Heart

I was stunned. In all my bustling and figuring and planning and finagling, God is working in the hearts of His people. When we pray that God will cause others to love Him more, He answers. I am the one who is looking for glory and power, outward evidence. But here was my husband, steady, faithful, and courageously believing for the goodness of God. The unrelenting goodness that pursues us and transforms us from the inside out. May we have this kind of courage.

As you spend your days either whispering or breathing up momentary prayers or carving out time for on-your-knees intercessory prayers, may you begin to cultivate the courage to pray the biggest, scariest prayer: "Lord, let them love you more. Let them seek You and Your goodness rather than Your glory." The beautiful thing that I am starting to see, after years of praying this way, is that when I am praying for others this way, it changes me as well. Those square inches of my heart that God is fighting for begin to giveaway under His beautiful, unrelenting, pursuing love. Have courage to pray.

Chapter Four

Courage to Lament

"Let everything happen to you
Beauty and Terror
Just keep going
No feeling is final"
—Rainer Maria Rilke

Recently my cousin and I met up at my mom's home for a short but sweet little reunion. Having grown up with only brothers, my two girl cousins became more like sisters and were an integral part of my childhood. As we were visiting, the topic of mental health came up and we were discussing various counseling styles we had tried or heard about. We landed on trauma therapy for a bit, at which point she declared, "Yeah, trauma isn't really a thing for me." Without skipping a beat, I agreed.

"I know what you mean. I'm sure I need some kind of counseling, but I don't think I have a problem processing trauma."

Sometimes, and I don't think this is irreverent, I am sure God is literally laughing at the dumb stuff we say. At the very least, He is shaking His head. For my cousin and me, it would take a few months before we had a hearty laugh over our very un-self-aware declarations. In that span of time between the brash statements of being expert trauma processors, we had both begun unraveling our pasts with abusive experiences and unhealthy church dynamics. We had been messaging each other; "Do you remember this?" "Can you listen to this podcast? It describes my experience." "What?! *That* happened to you?"

After weeks of messaging, we finally talked on the phone and recounted those fateful and deluded words from my mom's condo. After all our collective trauma, how could we think we had, somehow, gained the ability to process all of it in a healthy way? Granted, much healing has been done but to say, "processing trauma is easy for me" is a massive stretch. I have come to learn that trauma is an often-misunderstood word. Although it can be big and horrifying events that happen to individuals, a psychologist explained to me that trauma is essentially anything that the brain found overwhelming and was, therefore, unable to process.

Hiding or ignoring trauma is naturally what our brains do. It has been designed for all manner of self-preservation in order to avoid pain and discomfort, even if that means we have a whole lot more work to do in "garbage removal" years later. On one hand, pain avoidance can be a good thing. If our brains didn't shut down the processing during moments of significant pain or struggle, none of us would get anything done. For example, if a loved one dies, at some point, you still must take care of your kids, go to work, or get groceries.

But humans have taken this to an entirely other level that, if undealt with, can lead to many unwelcome mental, emotional, and physical manifestations.

In his famous book *The Body Keeps the Score*, Bessel van der Kolk explains, "Traumatized people chronically feel unsafe inside their bodies: The past is alive in the form of gnawing interior discomfort. Their bodies are constantly bombarded by visceral warning signs, and to control these processes, they often become expert at ignoring their gut feelings and in numbing awareness of what is played out inside. They learn to hide from their selves."[10] (p.97). Undealt with trauma doesn't just go away on its own, regardless of how many times we bully ourselves to "get over it" or "forget about it."

The first time I was presented with irrefutable evidence that the body does keep the score was during the first most devastating moment of my adulthood. I received an unforgettable phone call from my devastated mother, saying that my parents' marriage was tragically ending. I still remember sitting in shock on the edge of my bed while my two little girls giggled in the other room. The contrast was jarring.

Although my parents' marriage had been difficult, this was not how I pictured it ending. I was twenty-nine years old and suddenly felt like a scared child who just wanted to hide behind the bedroom door until everything was safe for me to come out. But that is not what survivors do, right?

Like a veteran trooper, I marched into the following weeks carrying on business as usual. I fielded phone calls from various family members. Trying to encourage and remain

---

10 Kolk, Bessel van der. *The Body Keeps the Score: Mind, Brain and Body in the Transformation of Trauma*. London, U.K.: Penguin Books, 2015.

strong and functioning. I was fine. I would be fine. I broke down somewhat with my husband but made sure no one else saw tears or weakness. But God did not design our beings to withstand this kind of dishonesty. And that is what I have come to see this kind of faux bravery as, dishonest. There is a reason that Shakespeare's "the truth will out" resonates so deeply with readers throughout the ages.

The fact that our bodies will revolt when we are not looking at and dealing with our emotions is something I have come to find both hilarious and irritating. But ultimately, valuable because it reminds us that our God does not want us to remain in grief and pain but to be transformed by it, as we see at the beginning of the book of James. (James 1:2-4)

During the early stages of this nightmarish time in 2002, the first sign that all was not well with my soul was waking up with hives. Yes, a lovely red rash from out of nowhere. Red, prickly itchy, covering my torso and making me irritable. I was so unaware of the impact of trauma on the physical body that I went to the doctor expecting her to diagnose a new allergy or send me for bloodwork.

She took one look at the rash and queried, "So, have you been experiencing a significant amount of stress lately?" And that began a very long journey toward discovering the power that unchecked and unacknowledged emotional pain can have on our entire being. Up until this point, my twenty-nine-year-old self was truly ignorant of the fact that emotions, brain, and body were connected in that integral way. I had become the queen of compartmentalizing, but my body couldn't keep up anymore.

Everywhere we turn, we're told that getting over things and moving on is the brave thing. We are told that trauma is

Courage to Lament

only the big ugly abuses and events, but it can be anything that our brain finds too overwhelming to process or make sense of in a helpful manner. From being teased as a child to finding out my parents' marriage had been obliterated, not treating everything that I encountered as worthy of my attention was not brave. As Bessel van der Kolk states: "As long as you keep secrets and suppress information, you are fundamentally at war with yourself...The critical issue is allowing yourself to know what you know. That takes an enormous amount of courage."[11] And there it is. Courage. Courage to look at your crap. Courage to admit that it happened and that it was hard, and courage to integrate it into your life story as God intended.

Unfortunately, it is not just society at large that promotes this kind of pain avoidance. Much of the church has also become master at faking happy and moving on, even though the Bible is packed with teachings on a God who invites our full range of emotions. The degree to which even mature and educated Christians have gone to cover up and twist this beautiful teaching is astonishing. I have lost track of how often I have heard a Bible teacher say, "even though the Psalmist can be crying out to God, expressing doubts and fears, he always ends with praise." Always. And if I'm going to be fair, I perpetuated that teaching for more years than I am comfortable to admit.

While this is true for most Psalms, it is certainly not true for all. It is not *always*. I was somewhat gob-smacked when someone first pointed out that the Psalmist does not always land in a happy place by the end of his writing.

---

11 Kolk, Bessel van der. *The Body Keeps the Score: Mind, Brain and Body in the Transformation of Trauma.* London, U.K.: Penguin Books, 2015.

The invitation for us to truly lament, to sit in and feel all the pain and hurt of a situation, is a strong current throughout scripture, and yet, in over 30 years of sitting under hundreds of sermons, I have heard next to nothing on this topic. "Most Christians do not think they have permission to consider their feelings, to name them, or express them openly. This applies especially to the more 'difficult' feelings of fear, sadness, and anger… When we deny our pain, losses, and feelings, year after year, we become less human. We transform slowly into empty shells with smiley faces painted on them."[12]

The fact that we have been so heavily indoctrinated to steer clear of the concept and doctrine of lament is evident in my ability to spend years hiding out in the Psalms and still not seeing that the teaching "all Psalms end in praise" is a myth. I know that it is very encouraging to see the full progression of another Christian, whether a Psalmist or a friend, move from deep grief, loss, and disappointment to the arrival of newfound joy and praise. But when the time finally comes for your first dark night of the soul, you will discover that this progression is not a sure and rigid formula with a linear trajectory.

In these desperate moments, it will bring great comfort for you to know that giants of the faith have sat in the muck and mire of pain and doubt without any end in sight, and you will want to know that the honest cries of "how long, O Lord?" are not sinful or signs of weakness. It is in these moments that you are saying yes to God. You are saying yes to lament. Ultimately, you are saying yes to being changed in deep ways that require more courage than you can imagine.

---

12 Scazzero, Peter. *Emotionally Healthy Spirituality – it's Impossible to be Spiritually Mature, While Remaining Emotionally Immature.* Grand Rapids, MI: Zondervan, 2017.

Courage to Lament

Thirteen years after my parents' divorce, I was faced with the grief of my father's death. As I have already shared, due to a history of abuse and possible unrepentant heart from my dad, it was a very complicated grief. But I had years of learning the importance of not running from the big feelings, so I was able to catch myself when I was doing this. I received support, grace, and care from those around me. I had the words to communicate with my husband when I either needed time alone or time with him while he sat in my grief with me.

I also felt more comfortable setting boundaries when I needed to retreat from others. Sometimes, this meant canceling plans with friends or acknowledging when I didn't feel safe enough to have a raw conversation with someone. One of the best pieces of advice I was given soon after my dad died was from the school counselor where I worked at the time. Jan was primarily there for the elementary students, but she often invited staff into her little cubby-hole-sized office for respite and wisdom.

During one such session, she told me that to grieve in a healthy manner, one must schedule it. For example, after the death of a loved one, once the feelings have grown less raw, you may think that you are now ready to get back into circulation; going about the daily routine, back to work, etc. But there is still pain waiting for you in deep places. She suggested that, instead of that pain coming out at very inconvenient times, like when the cashier at the grocery store asks you how your day is going, you are proactive. If you set aside a few evenings a week at a particular time to be with your grief (I know, it sounds macabre) and process it on your terms, you will be able to come through the "valley of the shadow" in a healthy way.

Like everything God requires of us or instructs us in, lament is good for our souls and our entire being, including our physical bodies. The study of neuroscience has confirmed repeatedly that what happens in our minds impacts our bodies. Properly acknowledging, processing, and sorting our emotions is not unlike cleaning and ordering our home. When we have taken the time to properly file our important papers, put clothes in the correct drawers, and throw away the excess, we have a much greater measure of peace and enjoyment in our daily lives.

However, in a hurried and harried culture that encourages us to be strong and stoic we have no opportunity to properly process grief and disappointment and it remains with us like an untidy junk drawer, ready to spill out at any random moment.

When we call a funeral a "Celebration of Life," we declare that grieving is unnecessary and unwelcome. And far worse, we inadvertently convey the notion that God is also uninterested in hearing our cries and questions in the painful and confusing moments. It's as if we have been told, "don't bother God. He's too busy to listen to your lament." We are at risk of making a god in our own image.

In *A Grief Observed*, C.S Lewis walks us through his own grief after losing his beloved wife. He gets to the heart of the true problem: "Not that I am (I think) in much danger of ceasing to believe in God. The real danger is of coming to believe such dreadful things about Him. The conclusion I dread is not 'So there's no God after all,' but 'So this is what God's really like. Deceive yourself no longer.'"[13] It is,

---

13 Lewis, C. S. *A Grief Observed.* New York, NY: Seabury Press, 1980.

therefore, crucial to study the way God wants to be known amid grief.

The moment in recorded history that resounds with the most beauty, courage, and honesty in lament is Jesus raising Lazarus from the dead. Only found in the gospel of John, I find myself turning to this story frequently when I want to be reminded of the character of the God I follow. Since I can become so familiar with famous Biblical stories, I find it crucial to slow it down sometimes, sit on a dusty ancient road, and watch it all play out, observing the little details.

Jesus is walking down the road to Bethany days after his beloved friend, Lazarus, has died. John 11:5 says that Jesus didn't just love Lazarus but also his sisters, Mary and Martha, and he is expecting to comfort them upon his arrival at the tomb. But he is expecting something more: questions, confusion, and heart-wrenching grief. As the sisters draw near to Him, we watch two different responses. First, Martha appears logical and grounded: "Yes, Lord; I believe that you are the Christ, the Son of God, who is coming into the world." There is a neatness about Martha's response that our North American sensibilities tend to applaud. Well done, Martha, for taking Jesus at his word. This must be the only acceptable grief response, right? But then it's Mary's turn.

Her grief cannot be contained with words. After openly blaming Jesus for her brother's death, she simply throws herself in the dirt at Jesus' feet and weeps. Audacity or courage? The answer comes in what we see Jesus do next. For years I read quickly to "Jesus wept," but what comes before is life-altering. "When Jesus saw her weeping, he was deeply moved in his spirit and greatly troubled." (John 11:33) The term "deeply moved" has a sense of indignation attached to it, not indignation with Mary but with the whole ugly mess of sin and death.

This is not what was intended for the image bearers. Jesus is directly confronting not just Mary and Martha's grief but his anger and grief over the concept of sin and death for which he will soon be paying the ultimate punishment. And then "Jesus weeps." Right there. In public. On the road, we watch Him become the most vulnerable a human being can become. God becomes human in the fullest sense as he steps more fully into our grief than we can even step.

Once again, on the other side of courage comes relief and healing. Walking with our compassionate God through painful emotions leads us to discover that He does weep with us. He validates where no human could. I am slowly learning to pause with every disappointment, regardless of the size, and talk to Him about it while I try to feel all the things. I was always told this was wallowing, but it turns out it is integrating. It is a way of honestly putting all the feelings and thoughts where they need to go, and it is an opportunity to feel the care and comfort of a God who cares. Of a Savior who became incarnate to ensure He could identify with all of it; from a canceled concert you were looking forward to (true story), to the loss of a loved one.

He welcomes all your frustrations and all your questions, and when you are done, you will still find him there waiting to show you the resurrection life that is awaiting you because of Christ, just as he did for Mary and Martha. What I have discovered is that when you are His, when you know Jesus, and you allow yourself to be alone with Him to sit in your grief, He will be with you. If you have the courage to be honest and allow all the time you need, He will honor your presence and hear you.

Ultimately, that is the crux of it all: lament requires honesty before God, and honesty is terrifying. You will be reminded that there is no ache or pain that Jesus did not suffer. He will grieve with you if you have the courage to lament.

Chapter Five

Courage to Raise a Prodigal

"There's a wideness in God's mercy
I cannot find in my own
And He keeps His fire burning
To melt this heart of stone
Keeps me aching with a yearning
Keeps me glad to have been caught
In the reckless raging fury
That they call the love of God"
Rich Mullins - Love of God

"**W**hat if I WANT to go to hell?" A certain four-year-old daughter blurted out during family devotions many years ago, and I can still recall wondering what on earth I was supposed to do with that. I didn't grow up in an entirely Christian home, but I was pretty sure that this was not the result of good Christian parenting and very likely, how the Prodigal Son must have started out. Yikes. The famous parable of the prodigal son is found in Luke 15:11-32 and tells the story of a father with two sons: one who is faithfully and obediently working for his father and the other who dishonorably demands his inheritance now, while his father still lives, and takes off to live a recklessly hedonistic and destructive life.

He ends up squandering his significant inheritance on every passing pleasure and, after spending his fortune, finds that the only thing he is fit for is taking care of pigs and living in squalor as a poorly paid hired hand. The older son remains to do the dignified work his father has expected of him. If you were a parent, which son would you prefer?

I recently read a parenting article that described the story of the Prodigal Son as the story that strikes fear into the heart of every Christian parent. While we don't want to admit it, I believe that this is the response of most Christian parents. How can I avoid having a Prodigal Child? For a long time, I would have included myself in that category. Although I projected a laid-back demeanor towards parenting my four kids by laughing through the embarrassing moments or making self-deprecating comments, underneath the veneer was often distinct terror. What if we read the wrong parenting books? What if we made the wrong choice for education? What if we did our best to introduce Jesus to our children, and they still end up in a proverbial pig sty?

However, in the past year, as my children have marched, one by one, into adulthood, my thinking began to shift, and I finally realized that I had been in error. My former belief about the Prodigal Son betrayed a complete misunderstanding of God's generous and abundant heart for His children. It also betrayed a fundamental misunderstanding of the gospel as I focused more on the first half of the story and neglected the breathtaking end of the story. I had turned the story into a cautionary tale rather than what it is: a love story of the pursuing love of God the Father.

I finally came to see that obsessing on how I could avoid raising a prodigal kept me bound in fear, but coming to see that having the courage to *want* my children to be prodigals would lead me to a place of peace and trust as I began to understand what being a prodigal really means.

Admittedly, arriving at this epiphany was helped by the perspective of having years of parenting to reflect upon, along with the fact that young adult children no longer require your moment-by-moment intervention. Gradually, as the maternal strings were being clipped, with plenty of gentle encouragement from my husband, I gained some clarity. I also believe that the Holy Spirit had me dig into another story in the Bible that contrasted the prodigal in a surprising way. It was the tragic story of another famous son in scripture and not the one you may think. It wasn't the older, faithful son in the prodigal story who caught my attention.

Unlike the prodigal, this son was not a parable representation but an actual historical person. Unnamed but real all the same: The Rich Young Ruler. The nickname comes from patching the synoptic gospel accounts together. While all three of them say that he was rich, only Matthew states that he was young (Matthew 19:20), and Luke teaches that he was a ruler (Luke 18:18).

The combination of these adjectives tells us that he was likely a Jewish leader and teacher in the local synagogue; deeply instructed in the full teaching of the Mosaic law. Therefore, when he approaches Jesus, it is likely that he would have felt quite confident that Jesus would applaud him for his knowledge and status.

Tragically, he is in for the shock of his life as Jesus' words would fly straight as an arrow to the little kingdom of idolatry and self-righteousness that he has been building in the secret places of his heart. The young man begins to expose himself the moment he claims to have kept *all* the commandments. Like all of us, he is trying to bypass having a circumcised heart, a heart that has been torn apart and restored in the most beautiful way by the Father.

This young man is not coming with a need. He is not coming in humility our brokenness as God requires; "a bruised reed he will not break, and a faintly burning wick he will not quench." (Isaiah 42:3a) I think without even realizing it, the Rich Young Ruler is coming under false pretenses. His words are telling Jesus that he has a lack ("What must I do to be saved?") But he believes the opposite. He thinks he has something to offer which will earn him a gold star. When the apostle Paul shares his litany of earthly religious achievements in Philippians 3, one realizes that before his conversion, he could have been The Rich Young Ruler. He had all the impressive credentials for temple glory but was also capable of murdering the followers of Christ. Chilling.

With each reading, I became more and more uneasy about how little I had thought of this man in regard to raising children in the church. How is it, I began to ask myself, does the Rich Young Ruler not strike terror into the hearts of parents in the same manner as the Prodigal? Why do we tend to dread the possible prodigal child but spend very little time fearing the story that should really have us quaking in our boots? If there is fear to be had, it should be about him. I believe that the reason we, as parents, aren't keeping the

Rich Young Ruler on our parenting radar is that, secretly, we wouldn't mind being the parents of such a child.

It is extremely validating to be told that your child has won the award for the most memorized verses in Sunday School. Or that your child has been asked to be part of the worship team in the school chapel. And for those of us with single daughters, how many mothers would not want someone to introduce our young women to the Rich Young Ruler if he showed up in our church on a Sunday morning? Would we be listening to the warning of the Holy Spirit that he is a fraud or, instead, beam as he engages with the pastor on the finer point of doctrine? A caveat: doctrine is extremely important but, like anything, if it is used to impress then it is dangerous.

The truth is, we can get so caught up in downloading all the correct Christian information to our children that we forget that God wants their hearts and that can be messy business which will require the watching parent to have great courage. It usually takes a long time and is between them and God. It could involve pain and even a season of honest reckoning that lasts far longer than we would like.

It could mean a ten-year-old who is rude to a sweet elderly lady at church. It could mean that your son accepts a dare to throw food on the lawn of the neighbors who live next to the church (both true stories). But it could also be much more dark and painful than any of my words could convey over a much longer period of time than we can imagine.

Some of the Christian parents that I have come to admire most are those who have had to let their children go through dark and devastating paths and can only watch and pray with broken hearts. Unfortunately, it is far too common for parents to expect that raising their children in the faith is like a transaction. I do this right thing and God is required to give me a nice polite Christian child.

I have lost count of the number of times a Christian mother has uttered, in bewilderment, "How could my child have done that? They were raised in a Christian home!" I confess, there have been moments when I, too, have felt ripped off by my children's actions. They had so much more than I had growing up, in terms of spiritual instruction and gospel exposure. Why weren't they better? Or, rather, why weren't they making me look better? That is often the problem. The hard truth is that in our attempt to modify our children's behavior to a level that would impress a watching world, we can be getting in the way of the beautiful and hidden work that God is intending to do in them.

Teaching our kids self-sufficiency, grit, and resiliency can also teach them to live like "practical atheists" as I have heard a pastor say; people who claim to be reliant on the work of the Holy Spirit in their lives but, in practice, lean on their own human resources and faculties. Having the incredible courage to let your children be a bit messy and giving them space to figure things out with God, even from a fairly young age can have beautiful long-term results. In *Courage to Stand*, Russell Moore explains the myth behind the well-behaved or resilient child. "Often these super-resilient children fall apart midlife. The child needed to grapple with the crises of childhood– not just to hide behind people-pleasing or performing for a demanding parent– to navigate the crisis coming later on."[14]

One of the unforgettable gifts that the Lord gave my husband and I early on in our parenting was the story from

---

14   Moore, Russell. *The Courage to Stand: Facing Your Fear Without Losing Your Soul.* Nashville, TN: B & H Publishing, 2020.

a visiting pastor that he shared in his sermon. The pastor described how a member of his congregation approached him with a rebuke. This man was, essentially, scolding this pastor for the behavior of his children who were then preteen and early teen aged.

Initially the pastor adopted the apologetic countenance of embarrassment and was agreeing with the parishioner. But then the pastor realized that what this man was describing was not actually grievous sin or even wild rebellion like burning someone's barn down or throwing rocks at the neighbor's windows. They were acting like the immature humans that they currently were. The pastor made the courageous choice and said no. No, his kids were still kids and needed a lot more time. Many years, in fact, to grow into mature people. He was allowing for time that the slow and authentic work of growing up requires.

Regardless of our own exposure to scripture and teaching, it is so easy to lose sight of the fact that we have a God who "looks at the heart" (1 Samuel 16:7). Afterall, behavior modification is not the same as sanctification. In the Rich Young Ruler, we see the former; a disciplined knowledge of and adherence to the law which gave him the appearance of one with all of heaven to gain. But ultimately, it is the Prodigal son who ends up with the prize. He does all the wretched stuff that a good Christian kid is not supposed to do but he finds Christ. He sees his need for a savior, and he runs into the reckless love of God. I love Tim Keller's teaching on this moment in *The Prodigal God:*

"The *prodigal* does not mean "wayward," but, according to the Merriam-Webster Collegiate Dictionary, *"recklessly spendthrift."* It means to spend until you have nothing left. The term is therefore appropriate as used for the father in the story as for his younger son. The father's welcome to the repentant son was literally reckless because he refused to "reckon" or count his sins against him or demand repayment.... In this story the father represents the Heavenly Father Jesus knew so well. St. Paul writes, "God was in Christ reconciling the world to Himself, not reckoning to them their trespasses" (2 Cor. 5:19 ASV). Jesus is showing us the God of great expenditure, who is nothing if not the prodigal to us, his children. God's reckless grace is our greatest hope, a life-changing experience."[15]

I love this description of the prodigal God. But often we are so stingy and fearful when it comes to showing this kind of God to our kids, let alone this kind of love to our kids. Countless times the heart of the reckless, prodigal God has been there to remind me that the gospel is free. The shame can go, the chains are off, and I can breathe in the free air. But I still tended to show a different face to my children.

I found myself encouraging them to make fail safes. How much are you reading your Bible? What do you look like at church? How many Bible studies are you attending? What Christian podcasts are you listening to? Just in case you needed this advice: young adults are not generally interested in watching/reading/listening to all the stuff a middle-aged

---

15 Keller, Timothy. *The Prodigal God: Recovering the Heart of the Christian Faith.* New York, NY: Penguin Books, 2016.

mom is into. Plus, shock of all shocks, the Holy Spirit is for them as well and will put good things in their path without *any* of your help. As in none. No help.

I have seen too many children leave their faith in tragic and painful ways for me to glibly say that I would gladly watch my child walk through the modern-day equivalent of the Prodigal Son journey rather than maintain an outward appearance of righteousness. I do not believe that a child growing up in a Christian home is required to experience a period of self-destructive rebellion to come to faith. But what I am praying for with my kids is a true and honest knowing of the person of Christ. I am seeking to know and delight in the Father so that my words, when required, won't be hollow.

My heart's desire is that my husband and I will understand the rich and generous heart of God in order to have the courage to emulate that to our children. Simultaneously, I am seeking to rest in the truth that the results are completely out of my power or control. Without question, that is the hardest and scariest journey a parent must walk. There is free will. We can't flip a 'believe' switch on for our kids. But even there, we find comfort as God our Father understands this more than we ever could and, as He did for you and me, can pursue them with a beautiful and reckless love.

As Lore Ferguson Wilbert points out, "Behavior modification - simply acting differently - wasn't the aim of our life in Christ. Christ has strong words for those He calls 'whitewashed tombs' (Matt. 23:27), painted houses of death, because they were evidence of having the right presentation but the wrong motives. The heart of the problem for Adam and Eve, and for you and me, is that we are sinners in need of a Savior. And if the bad news is that we are all unclean, the good news is that there is one gospel to cleanse us from *all* unrighteousness. But before we can get to the heart of the problem, we have to name the problem, we have to name the problem of the heart."[16]

May we have the courage to seek the highest calling for ourselves and our children; to encounter the living Christ and allow Him to change us from the inside out. The Prodigal Son was transformed because he understood the character of the father. Parents, instead of comparing our children and focusing on the outward, let us remind each other that it is about the heart. And run recklessly and fearlessly into the arms of God.

---

16 Wilbert, Lore Ferguson. *A Curious Faith: The Questions God Asks, We Ask, and We Wish Someone Would Ask Us.* Grand Rapids, MI: Brazos Press, a division of Baker Publishing Group, 2022.

Chapter Six

Courage to Trust

"Howling ghosts, they reappear
In mountains that are stacked with fear
But you're a king and I'm a lionheart"
Of Monsters and Men - *King and Lionheart*

Last week I had one of my gospel playlists running in the background. Feeling shaky with the reality of several difficult situations, I needed whatever encouragement the well-worn songs could offer. Halfway through a new variation of *Tis So Sweet to Trust in Jesus*, I suddenly skipped the song with a bit of irritation. I paused what I was doing to check in on the agitation creeping through my body. *No, it's not,* I thought, *it's not sweet to trust in Jesus. It's absolutely terrifying.* It is with a good measure of vulnerability that I admit that this was not the first time I have had this thought.

Several times over the years, when facing scary circumstances, it has felt even more frightening to intentionally trust God with the outcome. The first time I remember coming face to face with this honest response to putting my trust in an invisible God was almost nineteen years ago.

Take Courage, Dear Heart

Although not the first time that I really needed to trust Him, it was the first time I remember having the courage to voice my struggle. Simply put, I didn't want to place my life or my child's life in the hands of God.

It was January 2005 when my baby, my fourth and final, was only two weeks old. It was bleak mid-winter, and a respiratory virus was wreaking havoc on young babies in the area where we lived, and my little girl was sick. Since she was my fourth, I felt as though I had seen or, at least heard of, all the symptoms and illnesses. I had been confident that since we were living in the 21st century, flu wasn't something to fear in a healthy human, even if she was a less than nine-pound human. But there she was, feverish and agitated, barely interested in feeding. It was right around bedtime for the older three kids that I heard of a local baby who died of what my daughter was suffering from. Died.

My husband and I were giving each other pained and confused looks and I was taking slow deep breaths to keep calm when a friend called. After telling her in a faltering voice what was happening and that I was probably going to take my Abigail to the ER, she made the innocent statement: "Sheen, you just have to trust the Lord."

I can still see where the paint was chipping on our little wooden kitchen table. I stared at the sage green and paused. Finally, I responded, "Yes. But that means trusting Someone who I also believe has the power to, not just save, but also take my baby." I could hear the emotion in my friend's voice as she held that reality with me for a moment and then quietly said, "Yes. I'm so sorry."

I sat up with my baby for a couple more hours trying to either feed her or soothe her to sleep. When I could do neither I had my husband help me pack up a bag, bundle up my baby and headed to the ER while he had to stay back with our other sleeping children. Up until that moment, any visit to the emergency room for me had always involved a certain amount of waiting. Occasionally we had had a child with an asthma attack that got us through triage a bit quicker than a potential broken bone. But I can assure you that I was utterly unprepared for what happened when I arrived at Children's Hospital with Abigail.

Arms laden with a newborn in a car seat and an overflowing diaper bag, I was quickly ushered straight past the triage counter, and, with complete calm and composure, the attending nurse had whisked my baby out of my arms and into a room I had never seen before. In under five minutes her tiny body was on a bed that looked gigantic in comparison, and she was hooked up with IV and an oxygen mask.

Historically, I am a fight over flight person. I don't fall apart. I am strong. I don't faint and I don't panic. But the professionals in that room suddenly saw a terrified and shaking mother breathing heavily from shock. A chair was rolled under my knees seconds before they were about to collapse. I leaned on the table beside me trying not to hyperventilate while the nurses told me that we would be admitted and would not be going anywhere any time soon. Somehow, I was able to ask for a phone so I could call my husband. I can only imagine what it would have been like for Vern to be at home, unable to comfort me properly or to see his baby.

The rest of that day was a blur of bloodwork and monitors and repeated conversations with doctors and interns. She was sick. Really sick and there was no way of guaranteeing anything, they told me. My memory from that first day in the hospital does not gain clarity until the nighttime. That first sleepless night – my second in a row – will be forever embedded in my memory. We were in a hospital room by ourselves. Nurses were coming and going, and specialist respiratory doctors came to perform procedures on Abigail that would enable her little body to get more oxygen. But it was in the in-between times that God and I had it out.

My chair was pulled up to the hospital bed so that I could lay my head on the bed while stroking my baby's body and simultaneously holding a soother in her mouth because she was too agitated to sleep and too weak to nurse. The prayers began more like internal screaming at God; *I cannot trust her to you because you might take her. You cannot take my baby because I will die.* To which I had a very clear voice in my head, again, more of a thought that was not my own, *No. You will not die.* To which I countered with my original argument. And repeat. For hours. *I will die. No, you won't.*

There were a few brief periods wherein Abigail drifted off to sleep but I could not. I just sat back in my chair and continued the wrestling match with God. It is difficult to describe but after hours of scream-praying and crying before the Lord an inhuman peace flooded over. It was about four or five in the morning, and I became distinctly aware that I loved God. I loved Him and believed that He was enough. He was more to me than my husband and more to me than my children. And while the reality of losing them would produce incalculable heartbreak, I would not die. Ultimately, I realized that the thought of walking away from my Savior would be infinitely worse. He was good. He was kind. He was trustworthy.

And so, I sat until the morning had fully arrived. Staring at my beautiful girl, still with a lot of fear, but with a different kind of hope and settledness. After another night where the nurses would tell me later, Abigail's life was very fragile, she finally turned a corner and after a week in the hospital, we were able to go home to the love and relief of our little family. There were endless cuddles and cozy blankets and rescuing baby Abigail from being hoisted around the house by toddlers.

I felt deeply grateful for the indescribable blessing of a healthy baby. But I also felt thankful for the intimate work that God had done in my heart. I am keenly aware of the fact that because I left the hospital with a recovering baby, I will never really know how I would have reacted if the worst had happened. But I also knew that a small transformative work had begun.

Looking back now I believe that what I had discovered in that dark night of the soul was courage. Courage that came through an honest reckoning with a gracious and benevolent God who can handle the inner wrestling of His children. Repeatedly, this is the recurring piece that I am seeing in the puzzle which is godly courage. "Trust the Lord", a common refrain in Christian communities is not helpful unless the person who requires the trust also has a solid grip on the person of Christ.

The phrase, meant to encourage, only resonates if the recipient is placing their trust in the person and not merely trusting in the outcome. If this is the case then, yes, we can affirm that it is altogether sweet and comforting to trust in Jesus. However, when I have been faced with outcomes that had the potential to be distinctly devastating, getting to the place of trust has involved a great amount of wrestling with God. The answer will always lie in the fact that there is an inextricable link between courage and an intimate connection to God. I am starting to wonder if "have courage" is synonymous with "come unto me" that we hear in Matthew 11:28-30.

I recently had someone tell me that in all the years that she had been told that Jesus was the Good Shepherd, what she had been picturing was a shepherd who was more of a drill sergeant walking behind her and prodding her little sheep body to *move, hurry up, stop going the wrong way!* In angry and impatient tones. As she was describing this inaccurate mental picture of the character of Christ, I realized how much I could relate to this in God's call for me to courageously trust Him in overwhelming circumstances and that there is a direct correlation between my lack of understanding of the person of Christ and my ability to trust Him.

"All true knowledge of the Savior is both necessary and useful for our enjoyment of God. To the degree that we know Jesus Christ, we shall know God. To the degree that we misunderstand our Lord, we shall be ignorant of God. Ignorance is no friend of spiritual growth. Jesus is the visible image of the invisible God (Colossians 1:15), so that those who see Jesus see the Father (John 14:9). No one can claim to truly know God who does not truly know his Son."[17] In the full article Mark Jones goes on to describe how at the incarnation Jesus became fully human and fully God for the rest of time. Thus, allowing Him to also fully sympathize with our weaknesses (Hebrews 4:14-16), retaining all power and

---

17   Jones, Mark. "Christ Confusion." *Desiring God*, 2020. https://www.desiringgod.org/articles/christ-confusion.

Courage to Trust

authority over all things, as well as giving us full access to God the Father. Again, knowledge of the person we are trusting is crucial.

As seen throughout the New Testament, Matthew 11:28-30 reveals the beautiful tenderness of Jesus. After thanking His Father for His followers, weak and faulty though they may be, He beckons them with, "Come to me, all who labor and are heavy laden, and I will give you rest. Take my yoke upon you, and learn from me, for I am gentle and lowly in heart, and you will find rest for your souls. For my yoke is easy, and my burden is light." When He desires for us to trust Him in all things, we are reminded that He is still doing the heavy work, the burden-bearing, of our lives. But even beyond this type of gentle beckoning the jarring reality is that Christ, Himself, found that He was required to wrestle in the same tug-of-war fashion to trust or not trust His Father.

It is after the heartbreaking prayer in the Garden of Gethsemane discussed in Matthew 4 that we see the resolve of Christ to walk through the valley of death on our account; darker than anyone could ever know, with a deep solemnity but also with the trust that comes after an honest dealing with and crying out to the Father. The road to Golgotha is still ahead of Him with all the horrors He knows are coming but the chief point is that he has moved out of the garden. He is proceeding with the plan. Something has shifted after the excruciating prayer, and He is willing to trust what lies before Him.

Again, we see the perfect example of what it means to live, and even die, for God: "There's a sense in which Jesus shows us what it means to live a fully dependent life upon God. Could He have chosen to rely directly upon His own divine nature? Of course. But that misses the point of His true servanthood. He came as God's servant, to do God's will, and to do the work given to Him on God's terms. In response, God the Father fitted and equipped Him to serve Him."[18] It is this kind of courage that I long for when I am faced with a potentially scary outcome. The courage to fully comprehend the difficult road ahead, the courage to wrestle in prayer, and then the willingness to trust.

As I am writing this chapter, our family is experiencing some big unknowns in the areas of health, employment, direction, and finances. After experiencing months of peace about these issues, about a week ago I found myself gripped with fear, to the point of panic, over how these circumstances could possibly be rectified or all the ways they could get horribly worse.

Thankfully, after a day or two of heart-racing anxiety, I was able to remember that night, years ago, of wrestling and that when I am afraid and need courage to trust God for whatever outcome, I can go to Him. I can admit that I am so afraid that if I trust Him, He might not give me the thing I want. It seems that the simple, faltering, act of "Lord, I believe but help my unbelief" (Mark 9:24) is enough to find myself, once again, drawn into His kind presence. I am still struggling daily with fear of the unknown but find that I am slowly coming to the place again of affirming that, yes, it is so sweet to trust in Jesus because He is altogether lovely and sweet in and of Himself. I am trusting in Him and not the outcome and gradually the peace is returning.

---

18   Jones, Mark. "Christ Confusion." *Desiring God*, 2020. https://www.desiringgod.org/articles/christ-confusion.

Chapter Seven

Courage to Release Resentment

*"Never be so polite, you forget your power
Never wield such power, you forget to be polite"*
Taylor Swift - *Marjorie*

One of the things I love about teaching is watching the way a kid's brains work. To be fair, the sheer immaturity of a ten- or eleven-year-old brain can occasionally cause me to internally scream, *what, in all that is good and holy, were you thinking?!?* while I fight to maintain my outer composure. But in the long journey to become an adult we lose a lot of sweet and sublime ways of looking at the world. One of these is the concept of having favorites. Kids have a lot more favorite things, and when you are their teacher, you are forced to think about all your little favorites as well.

"Mrs. Heinrichs, what's your favorite animal?"

"Eagle."

"What's your favorite color?"

"Green. It used to be blue, but now it's green." They will also want to know how and why this change occurred.

"What's your favorite season?"

"Summer."

"What's your favorite number?"

"Absolutely not." I tell the kids straight off that a favorite number is just not my thing. I can't do it. There are infinite options. But my favorite food, you ask? Cherries. Forever and for always, cherries. And it is with and surrounding cherries that I can recall my first experience with resentment and what it means to hold a grudge against someone.

Every summer as a child, my mom consistently bought or picked all the seasonal fruit in abundance. In June she would come home with a flat of perfect cherries: black-red, big, and firm. It was tradition on the first day the cherries came home to eat our fill of them. It was open season on cherries, and I exercised absolutely no restraint. It was the summer when I was about seven or eight when cherry day happened to coincide with a date night for my parents and the need for a babysitter for my brothers and me. Earlier in the day, we had eaten an unholy number of cherries and then watched as my mom put the rest of a, still decently full, flat of cherries in the fridge. More for tomorrow, my greedy eyes told me.

Unable to procure any of the usual babysitters, my mom asked a teen girl who we had never met before, a friend of a friend kind of thing. Fortunately, she came close to my bedtime because I could tell within a few minutes of her arrival that we were not going to be kindred spirits and bed looked like a better option than enduring the painful attempts at babysitter niceties from this new girl. Off I trundled, willing to get this day over with for more reasons than just babysitter avoidance. The sooner I slept, the sooner a new day with a new quota of cherries would arrive.

Courage to Release Resentment

As I entered the bright, perfectly 80's kitchen with orange cupboard doors, avocado fridge, and matching floral linoleum the next morning I could tell that my parents were rankled about something regarding the babysitter. *Cherries.* They were talking about the cherries. I quickly opened the fridge to discover that my precious flat of cherries had been decimated to a few scrappy stragglers strewn about the bottom; maybe five or six sad cherries littered amongst some pits and stems. I looked in horror at my mom for an explanation.

"I know! I can't believe it! After we left, she invited her boyfriend over, and they ate the entire box of cherries! We didn't notice until after she left."

I don't have a lot of memory of what I said or did. But I remember how I felt: Livid. I was angry and disgusted with this babysitter. I couldn't even appreciate the fact that, in different circumstances, I may have likely met my match in cherry love. A kindred, after all? But at the moment, the action of eating *all* a kid's cherries was on par with drowning kittens. Maybe one kitten. Maybe hurting a kitten. She got *paid* to eat all my cherries! My world was rocked. It wasn't as if I had never been disappointed or treated unfairly, which made my response a bit irrational and unexpected, but for years after, I would think back to her thievery with bitterness and disdain.

Of course, by now, the memory has become a funny one, something I was able to tell my children when they were little and loved mommy and daddy stories. They would be incredulous that a babysitter would do this and, simultaneously, entertained by the big reaction of a fuming little girl. Recently, though, I have sensed the faithful and niggling promptings of the Holy Spirit to address much bigger resentment and bitterness that I have quietly nurtured in the darker caverns of my heart and mind.

Resentment. Bitterness. It can come from anywhere at any time and can be the result of something truly hurtful and harmful, or it can stem from the innocent comment of a friend. A person may be truly vindictive in their treatment of you, or their presumptuous advice could leave you reeling. Adding insult to injury, you may even feel guilty for being upset because they clearly "meant well." Either way, left unchecked, the result is the same. Little tendrils start to make their way through your body, attaching themselves to your brain and heart, eventually sapping you of joy and strength.

From the unspecified tensions between Euodia and Syntyche mentioned in Philippians, to the murderous actions of Cain toward Abel, the Bible is clear that bitterness and resentment are destructive and, like all sin, lead to different levels of death. Resentment is generally considered to be the precursor to bitterness but both, when left undealt with, can wreak havoc on our well-being: spiritually, emotionally, and physically.

"Let all bitterness and wrath and anger and clamor and slander be put away from you, along with all malice. Be kind to one another, tenderhearted, forgiving one another, as God in Christ forgave you." (Ephesians 4:31) This verse, among many, makes it clear that bitterness is sin that will keep a measure of distance between God and us. Hebrews 12:15 reminds us that it is not something you can hang on to forever without it manifesting itself in ugly ways: "See to it that no one fails to obtain the grace of God; that no "root of bitterness" springs up and causes trouble, and by it many become defiled."

Courage to Release Resentment

Finally, there have been studies showing that any unchecked negative emotions, including bitterness, can lead to many physical ailments ranging from headaches and sleep loss all the way to high blood pressure and ulcers. As I peruse the evidence against hanging on to resentment and bitterness, I am increasingly aware of the contrast between what God desires for us and the meager existence we are so easily satisfied with. In Romans 2:4, God's call for us to repent is described as a kindness. While I tend to see confession of sin as something I am having to lose, this verse reminds me that I have far more to gain when I choose to repent.

While the word repentance conjures up fear and avoidance and a to-do list, it is the kindness of God who desires that we turn away from behavior and sin that offends a holy God and keeps us from living a whole and beautiful life. I believe that biblical repentance begins and ends with love. We are made aware that we are, in fact, sinning by the conviction of the Holy Spirit, given the desire to move away from it as well as the strength and ability to turn from it, and finally freed from it. And it is all the merciful work of a loving God through the complete work of Jesus Christ.

I love Tyler Staton's description of sin from his book *Searching for Enough*: "The trouble with sin isn't that God has a tight moral grid- and coloring within the lines is how we prove we're on his side. It's that sin inhibits us from doing what we were made to do- love. To minor on sin is to minor on love because sin constricts the capacity for love. Sin is a big issue to God because love is a big issue to God. If I pretend sin is a minor issue for me, I unintentionally make love a minor issue for me too."[19]

19   Staton, Tyler. *Searching for Enough: The High-Wire Walk Between Doubt and Faith*. Grand Rapids, MI: Zondervan Books, 2021.

Even after decades of following Jesus, I can still be suspicious of God when He requires me to give up my pet sins. Even when the Bible declares, "He who did not spare his own Son but gave Him up for us all, how will He not also with Him graciously give us all things?" (Romans 8:32) I can still feel like I am losing out when I need to truly repent, or turn away, from a particular sin. Like a pack rat who is guarding their junk as if it is a precious heirloom, I forget that I have riches beyond compare available to me in the forgiveness through Christ.

This desire to hold to something ugly when we have something infinitely more beautiful in store is perfectly described here by Henri Nouwen:

> "The resistance to praying is like the resistance of tightly clenched fists. This image shows the tension, the desire to cling tightly to yourself, a greediness which betrays fear. The story about an old woman brought to a psychiatric center exemplifies this attitude. She was wild, swinging at everything in sight, and scaring everyone so much that the doctors had taken everything away from her. But there was one small coin which she gripped in her fist and would not give up. If they deprived her of that last possession, she would have nothing more, and be nothing more. That was her fear. The man invited to pray is asked to open his tightly clenched fists and to give up his last coin. But who wants to do that? A first prayer, therefore, is often a painful prayer, because you discover you don't want to let go.

Courage to Release Resentment

You hold fast to what is familiar, even if you aren't proud of it. You find yourself saying: 'That's just how it is with me. I would like it to be different, but it can't be now. That's just the way it is, and that's the way I'll have to leave it.' Once you talk like that you've already given up the belief that your life might be otherwise, you've already let the hope for a new life float by. Since you wouldn't dare to put a question mark behind a bit of your own experience with all its attachments, you have wrapped yourself up in the destiny of facts. You feel it is safer to cling to a sorry past than to trust in a new future. So, you will fill your hands with small clammy coins which you don't want to surrender."[20]

Small, clammy coins. That image is unsettling, and, for me, became deeply motivating to see every bit of resentment and bitterness I was holding on to in this way; something worth giving up. Humans tend to project our miserly mindset onto God. When He is urging us to let go of the sin and walk into freedom and abundance, we can find ourselves snarling like Bilbo in The Lord of the Rings, when Gandalf demands that he hand over the ring of power; the very thing that was slowly killing Bilbo.

Even after looking at all the verses and even after admitting that these defiling offenders were damaging me and others, the question that plagued me was why did I not *want* to do the work of repentance? I was talking to a friend about this and right away she responded with, "Oh, because that's scary!" But after everything I just outlined regarding sin and God's

---

20 M., Nouwen. *With Open Hands*. Notre Dame, IN: Ave Maria Press, 2007.

delight to free us, what was I afraid of? The reality was that these resentments were offering me something. I had come to see them as a type of protection; something that would keep me from being exposed or vulnerable.

When we are sinned against, whether it is intentional or not, we are often left feeling like that person has taken something from us, leaving us weaker. Resentment steps in to offer us a form of validation and protection that feels good for a while. We feed it by reminding ourselves what this person did by carefully and painstakingly recreating their actions. We will very likely even tell others about the offense in an effort to bolster this counterfeit protection. As we receive validation from the other person, who we have now tainted with our resentment, we believe we have retained a bit of the power that we lost to the offending person. But as much as I prayed, I just couldn't get rid of the memories or the ugly emotions that bitterness invoked. I felt increasingly stuck and with the same amount of resentment.

At this point in my life, the resentments and areas of unforgiveness do not come from huge abuses but a lot of little things — the caustic or passive-aggressive comments that I was not ready for, the insensitivities and thoughtless actions of another. Like the "little foxes that ruin the vineyard" (Song of Solomon 2:15) they sneak in, usually undetected and too small to cause us great alarm. But like the root described in Hebrews, they take hold and begin to grow.

As a people-pleasing, Enneagram seven, Myers Briggs ENFP, extravert (did I cover all the things?), the way resentment building has looked for me is in the following way. I am in a conversation with a friend or acquaintance, and they say something that is unexpected or unkind. It might even

Courage to Release Resentment

come with a slight barb meant to convey the unforgiveness that person has towards me. I will usually feel the sting or prick immediately, and the other person may even have a fleeting look of regret.

What will I do? Probably laugh or joke to diffuse any potential tension. I will simultaneously be doing some quick self-talk along the lines of, "I'm probably imagining things" or "they couldn't have meant anything bad." Or I might have no idea what they meant but I'm not going to ask for clarification because that might make things awkward for a minute. The other person might even look a bit embarrassed by what they just said, but, apparently, it is my job to reassure them and redirect the conversation to put them at ease.

From the outside, this might look like graciousness, maturity, or kindness when it is dishonest and cowardly. I am simultaneously communicating to the other person that I have very low expectations for how they can treat people while telling myself that I do not possess the dignity, self-worth, or courage to speak up for myself. I would later ruminate on these conversations and, inevitably, feel like I had lost a little piece of myself. I wanted to forgive the person but the power I now held in creating resentment toward them made me feel safe, as if that would keep them from doing it again.

The conundrum of how to have the courage to forgive the person and repent of my bitterness while still retaining a sense of protection still held me bound. It wasn't until I finally remembered the words from a pastor. For years he had reminded the congregation that when the Lord is calling us to repent and give up a particular sin, He is wanting to replace it with something. But what was He wanting to replace the counterfeit safety of resentments with? Healthy boundaries.

Take Courage, Dear Heart

I believe that in having the courage to be honest and uphold healthy boundaries we can find legitimate security and move away from the lie that resentments will do anything good for us and finally be free of them. More than that, I believe that keeping healthy boundaries can be related to a Christlike love for others.

Boundaries have truly become a buzzword in our current culture and can be used as an excuse to cut anyone out of our lives who is slightly irritating or telling us things we don't want to hear, even if it could benefit us. However, there is a good and healthy way of viewing boundaries that can both honor yourself as an image bearer of the triune God as well as communicating love to those in your life. "Boundaries are expectations and needs that help you feel safe and comfortable in your relationships. Expectations in relationships help you to stay mentally and emotionally well. Learning when to say no and when to say yes is also an essential part of feeling comfortable when interacting with others."[21]

I appreciate how the author uses the word *safe* to describe how we feel with healthy boundaries. She uses that word again here: "Creating healthy boundaries leads to feeling safe, loved, calm, and respected. They are an indication of how you allow people to show up for you and how you show up for others." (pg. 8) Here we also see that it is connected to how well we can be available for others. Good boundaries are the opposite of selfish; they enable us to offer the better and more honest version of ourselves.

---

[21] Tawwab, Nedra Glover. *Set Boundaries, Find Peace: A Guide to Reclaiming Yourself.* New York, NY: TarcherPerigee, an imprint of Penguin Random House LLC, 2021.

Courage to Release Resentment

I think it is fair to say that Christians feel more obligated than others to say yes to everyone. Furthermore, it seems to me that it is Christian women who believe they cannot say no to anyone. They must always be willing and available to the needs of others without rest or reason. This tends to bleed into conversation where we believe that to be Christlike, we can never object to the way someone else is speaking to us or behaving toward us.

In the past I have even felt that I had to even let others dictate if we were going to be friends or not. I remember years ago a good friend rebuked me after she watched me turn myself into a pretzel to make an unhealthy friendship work: "Sheena, you don't have to be friends with everyone!" As a fellow teacher tells her students: "You don't have to be friends with everyone, but you need to try to be friendly." The idea of being "all things to all people" (1 Cor. 9:22) and "dying to ourselves" does not mean that we don't set kind and clear boundaries around our lives. I am slowly learning that there are a lot of awesome people out there, but we don't have time for everybody.

Somehow, we believe that we don't have the right to keep others accountable through healthy boundaries for fear of appearing unloving. The origin of this kind of thinking is confusing and, I'm sure, thoroughly analyzed elsewhere, but it is not found in the Bible.

While proving Himself to be the perfect example of grace, meekness, love, and sacrifice for humankind, Christ also showed us that, during His earthly ministry, He had boundaries. He pulled away from the crowds and even from His disciples several times. He even unapologetically pulled aside a few favorite apostles, showing us that it is not reasonable to expect that you will have the same type of relationship with everyone or that people are allowed access to you whenever they want.

I also find it fascinating that Paul also needed a break from Barnabas after they disagreed on whether Mark should accompany them on their missionary journey. (Acts 15:36-41) While the text said there was "a sharp disagreement," which is not ideal, at least there was no passive-aggressive guesswork going on. They simply parted ways, and later, there was full reconciliation. While this story may not be prescriptive, I think that it does show that even when not done perfectly, honestly conveying your opinion about something is better than stuffing it down in the hopes that others will just know or sense what is bothering you.

The hard reality is that there truly are horrible hurts and abuses that can be done to us. We may be required to not allow some people access to our lives for at least a period. It will very likely become necessary for you to need professional help to form good, clear, and safe boundaries that are healthy for you and your family. I believe that even during these times, we can seek to be free from bitterness and unforgiveness, even if it is someone that never needs to be in your life again. However, it is crucial to remember that it does not mean that to do that you can't have healthy boundaries. On the contrary, it will more likely be the component that enables you to walk through full repentance and freedom from bitterness.

Finally, when going through a time of repentance, I think it is important to remember the goodness of God and that He is a God who loves abundance, feasting, and parties. He is a God of more, not less. When we observe creation, we see more than enough: more flowers, more trees, more beetles,

Courage to Release Resentment

more birds, more fish, more beauty than we ever needed. Even more cherries. I have eaten more than enough cherries to make up for that missing flat in my fridge many years ago.

I believe that resentment and bitterness grow in the hearts of those who do not comprehend abundance. They flourish when combined with not being honest in our relationships and creating healthy boundaries. As we understand that God has so much more available to us, we can gain the courage to let go of all the stuff that keeps us captive, including resentment.

Chapter Eight

Courage to be Humble

*"To know oneself is, above all,
to know what one lacks. It is to measure oneself against Truth,
and not the other way around.
The first product of self-knowledge is humility . . ."*
—Flannery O'Connor

There is a distinct pattern that has surfaced in my life in relation to how God works something new in me. Because I have seen it clearly repeated several times, I can finally recognize it when it happens again. It starts out with me praying a simple prayer, usually while I'm reading my Bible. I will be aware of a general sin in my life. I will then pray, in bold generalities, for the Lord to remove this sin from my life. It is usually not a prayer of deep repentance or specifics which is, very likely, why the Lord has taken me on the soul-mining journeys that usually occur after the aforementioned vague prayers.

Essentially, I enter a period of weeks, months, or even years wherein I experience not more victory over the sin in question but less. Slowly and methodically, I become keenly aware of the depth of the sin and the specific ways it is manifesting in my life. It's a good time.

As mentioned in Chapter 8, it is not God's cruelty but kindness that leads us to repentance. And when we are attempting pseudo repentance which I am apt to do, He is more than able to work with that and do something that I have seen result in beautiful and lasting change in my life. Not perfection, but change.

One such occasion happened a few years ago after I attended a women's retreat where the topic was humility. The teaching, discussion, and prayer time were excellent, and I returned home wanting to learn more about the topic of humility but also with a sense of caution. At this point in my life, I had become aware of how my Apostle Peter impulsive style of praying had got me into trouble and thought I would try a slow and steady approach. But as the year chugged along, I was lulled into sneaky security and forgot the resolve to walk gently into new territory. I was reading through I Peter and came across Chapter 5, verses 6-7: "Humble yourselves, therefore, under the mighty hand of God so that at the proper time He may exalt you, casting all your anxieties on Him, because He cares for you."

At the time I read it, I was trying to quell some anxieties in my life and made the beautiful connection between trusting our fears to the Lord and humility. I was so distracted by this new-to-me revelation that I unwittingly did it. I made one of my big statement prayers; "Yes Lord! Make me more humble!" I even took it a step further: "Humble me under your mighty hand." Go big, right? And for me that meant whipping out one of my yellow cue cards, carefully writing out the verse and slapping it onto my bathroom mirror.

Without wanting to be disrespectful, in hindsight, it felt like all of heaven cried "Action!" and got to work, throwing me into a variety of embarrassing, surprising, and head-shaking scenarios. The reasonable person knows that's not what happened, but I'm trying to convey how it feels to be on one of these joy rides called humbling. Over the course of about two months, the number of embarrassing moments increased at an alarming rate. On one occasion, I was at a Bible study with my oldest daughter. At the end of the study, we broke off into groups of about eight to ten people to pray for one another.

My group was privileged to have a dear elderly man. Normally I would be grateful because of his strong and gentle wisdom but this evening I was in a bit of a state. I was tired and slightly irritated with a lot of anxieties. Rather than pray out loud with others I just wanted to sneak out the side door which would have been preferable considering what happened next.

As this lovely man began to share his prayer requests at great length and in thorough detail, my inner dialogue was spiraling. *Come on,* I thought, *stop talking. We get it!* I know. Awful. But it gets worse. Once everyone had shared their prayer requests and we bowed our heads, instead of relegating myself to just listening to the prayers since I was clearly not in good spiritual shape, I thought I would march right in with some quick prayers that would knock a bunch of the requests off the list so we could go home.

But the moment I did, the dear elderly man also began praying in his loud, rich, baritone voice without noticing that

I had already started as his hearing was no longer optimal. My eyes flickered open in time to see the others in a circle holding back laughter while respectfully keeping their eyes closed.

Slightly embarrassed, yet undeterred because, remember, I wanted to get home, I took the next opportunity to get this prayer time done and dusted. As soon as he was finished, I marched in again and started praying for the young married couple sitting beside me. This is a couple I knew reasonably well. They had been in my home, and I had spoken to the wife on many occasions - often deep, meaningful conversations. But as I began to pray for them, the oddest thing happened. I forgot their names. I was into the prayer enough that everyone knew which names I should be saying, but nothing. Blank. Silence.

My heart raced, and I could feel my face heat up. Trying to remain calm, I tilted my head to the left and opened my eyes wide enough to see the wife mouthing their names to me. I quickly mumbled the rest of the prayer, did some deep breathing until all was over, and slunk out with my daughter. As we walked to the car, I remember her declaring, "Wow, mom! Just wow!" And laughing her head off as I groaned in shame.

Other scenarios that played out during this time where I felt like all my flaws were on display were not as funny. A family relationship that I had prided myself on keeping together began to painfully unravel and gradually I began to feel aware that something bigger might be going on. But it wasn't until I was bedridden with a migraine and feeling wretched that I really started piecing things together. My husband came into our room to check on me and as I tried to put into words what I had been feeling for a while; like God's hand had been on me (I used those words), a little flash of yellow caught my eye from our ensuite bathroom. The verse. The mighty hand. The humbling. I groaned.

I think it needs to be said that I do not believe that God is a capricious character who enjoys batting around His children like little balls of yarn. But I do believe that, like a good Father, He will take us to the places we need to be to see our sin, in all its specifics, in order to repent. For the Lord is a faithful Father who corrects and reproves. "For the Lord disciplines the one he loves and chastises every son whom he receives." Hebrews 12:6. And His "mighty hand" is also a gentle hand. A strong hand. A hand to hold and to protect as well as to set limits.

I have come to view these drawn-out episodes as the Lord graciously just getting me to the starting point of repentance and then providing a way to sanctification and transformation. Again, not perfection. Because of my tendency to be impetuous and overzealous, it is his patient care that reminds me that the attribute I am looking for cannot be acquired or applied by next Tuesday. So, there I was, at the starting point, delving into the topic of humility with, well, a bit more humility, perhaps.

I learned that the first place to begin is to meditate on the importance that humility holds in the eyes of God. With seventy to eighty mentions of humility in the Bible, the verse that speaks to me with the most volume is also from 1 Peter 5: "God opposes the proud but gives grace to the humble." (1 Peter 5:5b) Here Peter is quoting Proverbs 3:34, a book of the Bible that is very prolific in its warning about pride. It states that, along with the dire warning of being opposed by the almighty God, pride has the potential to lead to disgrace

(Proverbs 11:2), destruction, and an overall bad reputation. Pursuing pride is like insisting on pushing upstream against the torrent of a mighty river. It is futile and self-defeating.

Not only are there plenty of explicit teachings on pride and humility in the Bible but there is also an abundance of examples of those who insisted on making life harder for themselves than they needed to. In all the stories of flagrant pride, I believe King Nebuchadnezzar takes the prize. By the time we get to the fateful moment in the Babylonian king's life in Daniel chapter 4, he has already seen vivid examples of God's mighty power.

At this point, King Nebuchadnezzar has heard Daniel, a faithful servant of the Lord, accurately interpret his dreams by the power of God and watched as Shadrach, Meshach, and Abednego walked into and out of a fiery furnace. After these events, the king had times where he briefly acknowledged the glory and power of the one true God. But it is only a year after this that he stands on the roof of his palace, surveying all that he rules, and declares, "Is not this great Babylon, which I have built by my mighty power as a royal residence and for the glory of my majesty?" (Daniel 4:30) God's response is swift and cuts deep. Essentially, Nebuchadnezzar is driven to insanity and forced to live like an animal in the wilderness for years.

At first glance, most of us in our regular lives cannot identify with the life of King Nebuchadnezzar nor consider ourselves in danger of replicating his display of atrocious arrogance. But as this brazen king kept popping up in my brain, the truth began to dawn on me. I became aware of my own little kingdom that I was declaring rulership over in the same power-crazed manner as Nebuchadnezzar. Meager as my kingdom may be in comparison, the heart attitude was the same. Control. Glory. If there were successes in our home, I would take credit for them. If there were setbacks or failures, I was spinning my wheels to find solutions while throwing just-in-case prayers heavenward.

If I am brave enough to be honest, I can see that I want to be the "sun and moon" for my family. The one with all the answers. The one who can provide direction and order in their lives. As my older children first entered adulthood, I remember catching myself as I thought, *if you would just let me plan things out for you, you would be fine!* At least I caught myself. Actually, my husband usually did. Unfortunately, this attitude extended to my husband and friends as well. Whether it was life choices, depressive thoughts, or, what I considered, unhelpful belief systems, I was there to set people on the right path.

God's gracious pursuit of me has meant that he has not left me in the arrogant state I found myself, but, slowly, over several years, I have sensed the Holy Spirit call me to have the courage to pull back and humble myself by watching Him take care of my family in ways that I could not have imagined. It has often been extremely painful and scary.

It is the proud heart that views the "mighty hand" as an imposition meant to thwart our will instead of what it is when we view it with humility, the hand of provision and love. At the end of Nebuchadnezzar's period of insanity, he was able to humbly acknowledge his rightful place before an awesome and holy God and respond accordingly: "Now I, Nebuchadnezzar, praise and extol and honor the King of heaven, for all His works are right and His ways are just; and those who walk in pride He is able to humble." (Daniel 4:37)

Just as the warnings against the proud are common in scripture, so are the encouragements and promises to the humble: grace from the Lord (James 4:6, 1 Peter 5:5), favor from the Lord (Proverbs 3:34, Isaiah 66:2), freedom from anxiety (1 Peter 5:6-7), honor (Proverbs 15:33), a good reputation (Proverbs 29:23), abundant peace (Psalm 37:11), and joy in the Lord (Isaiah 29:19). Once again, I found myself asking, if pride is so ugly and abhorrent and humility so beautiful and beneficial, why do I struggle so much to run towards it?

As with the struggle to let go of resentment in Chapter 8, there is a measure of fear involved. It is one thing to discover the demon, but summoning the motivation and the courage to kill it is another. The key to effectively finding victory over pride in my life was to replace it with humility. But the courage to do so came from a fuller understanding of Biblical humility.

We believe the lie that if we seek humility, we will become lesser versions of ourselves; we will lose a part of our unique identity. As resentment and bitterness give us a counterfeit form of protection, pride gives us a counterfeit sense of self and personal agency. Pride says that to be the person we were meant to be, we must assert ourselves at every opportunity and reject any notion that we should conform to a belief system or ideology. That is why fear can well up in us when we are called to become Christlike, millions of followers all conforming to the likeness of one person. Surely, this would result in a mindless army of homogeneous automatons. Sadly, one need only watch the latest documentary uncovering a scandalous cult to see this played out in the manner that God did not intend. Same outfits, same clothes, same hobbies, same abuses.

Wherever there are human attempts to either make their way to God or self, uniformity reigns. But this was not God's intention for his image bearers. In his infinite creativity, God is able to make an infinite number of unique individuals. It is sin, proudly seeking its own manifestation and glory that causes us to become less ourselves, not more. I have observed in myself that sin and the fruit of our sin is common, boring, and uncreative. "The more we let God take us over, the more truly ourselves we become—because He made us. He invented us. He invented all the different people that you and I were intended to be … It is when I turn to Christ, when I give up myself to His personality, that I first begin to have a real personality of my own."[22]

One need only observe the change in the early followers of Christ in the gospels to see that the closer they come to Him, they become more, not less. It's as if they begin to make sense; the gifts and abilities that were being squandered and running amok came into order and were put to good use. Peter is a wonderful example of this. At the beginning of Peter's story in the gospels, he routinely gets it wrong. He has a strong, bold voice but was continually using it at the wrong times. Even his bold actions and declarations were misplaced.

Finally, and tragically, it is Peter who, I am convinced, knew shame and humiliation more than any person- ever. After declaring undying loyalty to Jesus, he denies Him at Christ's most desperate moment. As Tyler Staton described

---

22 Lewis, C. S., Andrea Kirk Assaf, and Kelly Anne Leahy. *Little Book of Wisdom: Meditations on Faith, Life, Love, and Literature.* Charlottesville, VA: Hampton Roads, 2018.

Take Courage, Dear Heart

Peter's betrayal, "it is the most infamous moment of failure in all four gospels."[23]

But after the resurrection and ascension of Christ, we begin to see Peter differently. Not a different Peter, though. He has not been punished, silenced, or sidelined because of all his impulsive, ill-timed statements and actions. Because he finally has a true vision and understanding of who the living Christ is and has experienced the most beautiful forgiveness, his strengths and gifts are now useful. They make sense.

Peter was chosen to be the first preacher to proclaim the gospel of Jesus Christ. In his sermon, we see a Peter who is no longer muddled in his thinking. "This Jesus, delivered up according to the definite plan and foreknowledge of God, you crucified and killed by the hands of lawless men. God raised Him up, loosing the pangs of death, because it was not possible for Him to be held by it." (Acts 2:23-24) In this sermon, it is evident that Peter is no longer confused about the identity, purpose, and power of Christ.

Appropriately, it is also Peter who is the one to write about humility in 1 Peter. When he wrote the words in the passage, it is easy to imagine that he understood what it was to humble himself under God's mighty hand. Peter of the bold statements and impulsive gestures. Peter who said, "Lord! I will die with you!" And was then openly rebuked and publicly humiliated. Yes, he understood what it meant to be humbled and then how to humble himself. And he also experienced what it felt like to receive grace, forgiveness, restoration, and to be exalted at the right time.

---

23 Staton, Tyler. 2022. "From Belief to Knowledge". Portland, Oregon, April 24, 2022

Essentially, Peter understood that the crucial shift from the ingenuine self to the authentic self that God intended requires humbling but results in something so worthwhile as it enables us to know God more fully. "What we hunger for perhaps more than anything else is to be known in our full humanness, and yet that is often just what we also fear more than anything else. It is important to tell at least from time to time the secret of who we truly and fully are... because otherwise, we run the risk of losing track of who we truly and fully are and little by little come to accept instead the highly edited version which we put forth in hope that the world will find it more acceptable than the real thing."[24]

Because of the lies we believe about humility, we try to steer clear of it and make up all kinds of false ideas about what it looks like to justify our avoidance. C.S Lewis does a beautiful job explaining what humility does and *doesn't* look like:

> "Do not imagine that if you meet a really humble man, he will be what most people call 'humble' nowadays: he will not be a sort of greasy, smarmy person, who is always telling you that, of course, he is a nobody. Probably all you will think about him is that he seemed a cheerful, intelligent chap who took a real interest in what *you* said to *him*. If you dislike him, it will be because you feel a little envious of anyone who seems to enjoy life so easily. He will not be thinking about humility: he will not be thinking about himself at all."[25]

---

24 Buechner, Frederick. *Telling Secrets.* San Francisco, CA: HarperSanFrancisco, 2004.
25 1898-1963., Lewis, C. S. (Clive Staples),. *Mere Christianity: A Revised and Amplified Edition, with a New Introduction, of the Three Books, Broadcast Talks, Christian Behaviour, and Beyond Personality.* San Francisco, CA:

As in all griefs, temptations, sorrows, and struggles, we have the most perfect story available to us. This is the story of a mighty king. So powerful in fact, that he could create a universe-and in this universe, a world. With plants of every type and color, animals in every shape, size, and purpose. And even human beings who would inevitably betray Him. This king would willingly come as a baby to dwell among His creation and submit Himself to the most humiliating treatment imaginable. It would have been humiliating and mortifying if it was towards a mere human. But this king was the King of kings, the perfect and holy God.

There is no moment of humiliation or bad treatment from another person that you or I could experience that could even compare with the treatment of Jesus Christ. It was unjust at every point, and yet He bore it all on our behalf. "Have this mind among yourselves, which is yours in Christ Jesus, who, though he was in the form of God, did not count equality with God a thing to be grasped, but made Himself nothing taking the form of a servant, being born in the likeness of men. And being found in human form, He humbled Himself by becoming obedient to the point of death, even death on a cross." (Philippians 2:5-8)

Because Christ has gone before us, we can have the courage to pursue humility in our own lives. When someone tells us all about something we already know, we can imagine Christ spending years in the synagogue hearing his created beings teaching from his word. If we ever have to experience the difficulty of moving from a lovely home to a more modest dwelling, we can think of Christ leaving the glories of heaven to live here. "Look for yourself, and you will find

---

HarperSanFrancisco, 2001.

Courage to be Humble

in the long run only hatred, loneliness, despair, rage, ruin, and decay. But look for Christ and you will find Him, and with Him everything else thrown in."[26] In summoning the courage to pursue humility and turn away from pride, we will find so much more in return.

---

26   1898-1963., Lewis, C. S. (Clive Staples),. *Mere Christianity: A Revised and Amplified Edition, with a New Introduction, of the Three Books, Broadcast Talks, Christian Behaviour, and Beyond Personality.* San Francisco, CA: HarperSanFrancisco, 2001.

Chapter Nine

Courage to Receive Love

*"I wanna have friends that I can trust
That love me for the man I've become, not the man I was."*
The Avett Brothers

"**I** love you dearly." These are the words I hear at the end of every single voice message from my friend Ashley. A few years ago, I joined a little group of women online with the purpose of supporting each other in life and writing. We were from Oklahoma, Texas, New York, South Africa, and Canada. We would meet over Zoom to share what we were working on, give suggestions to those stuck in a rut, and sometimes pray for one another when life hit us hard. Over time, we all got busy with work and family commitments and found that our different time zones made Zoom meetings impossible.

But somewhere along the way Ashley from New York and I kept sending each other voice memos. Put quite simply, we were kindred spirits, laughing at the ridiculous, crying at the beautiful. We slowly got to know each other through frequent voice messages that lasted as long as fifteen minutes.

Take Courage, Dear Heart

Through a solid year of tears and laughter and praying for one another, we have become very close. Recently, after a week of being off grid, on a camping excursion, I was able to listen to a catch-up message from Ashley. She shared some exquisite answers to prayer mixed in with some wonderfully embarrassing moments that made me grin. And then, as always, she ended the message with a very heartfelt "goodbye - I love you dearly." I sat out on my back deck, staring at the trees, and just breathed in her final words.

Suddenly and surprisingly, I had tears rolling down my cheeks. I believed her. I refused to let any negative intrusive thoughts creep in, and I decided to believe her. Silencing the inner critics and basking in the love of a friend felt like an act of defiance. It felt wild and careless as my insecurities and failures and mess-ups tried to push to the forefront of my mind, *If Ashley only knew what I was really like...* No, I told myself, *just believe her.*

The fear and confusion around how we give and receive love are very complex and can have a massive impact on how we live in relationship with God and those he puts in our lives. I have been told many things about love in my years in the church: people naturally love themselves; they don't need to be encouraged to do that more; conversely, we can't really love others if we don't love ourselves; love is not a feeling but an act of the will. It's not that I can either defend or dismantle any of those statements; it's just that I have had difficulty applying them to my life.

I believe that what lies behind, both, my arrogant and bold bravado as well as my insecure and incessant need for reassurance is the same thing. In my most honest moments I must admit that it's difficult to believe that I could be truly loved. When I present as selfish, prickly, or entitled, I am protecting myself from the vulnerability required to allow myself to be loved. In the same way, when my need for validation is a bottomless pit, I do not truly believe that unconditional love is available to me.

Humans have the skill of distracting ourselves; through either virtue or vice, exercise or binge-watching, scrolling or reading, serving or ministering, we will do a variety of things to avoid silence. Of course, somewhat overstated, there is some truth in Blaise Pascal's famous quote: "I have discovered that all the miseries of men derive from one single fact: that they cannot sit quietly in their own room." Sitting alone in silence, all the thoughts, fears, insecurities, pressures, and resentments can come creeping in like cold mist.

I remember my last year of university. Most of my friends had already graduated so I had decided to forgo dealing with unknown roommates and rented a very cool bachelor suite in a restored pink stucco heritage building. Originally an Art Deco mansion, the entrance contained a grand staircase, geometric woodwork, and abstract stained glass. Even my little apartment was lovely with high ceilings, huge windows, and an oversized fire escape that doubled as a patio that I could crawl out onto.

As beautiful as it was, the problem was, it was quiet, and it was one of the darker emotional times of my life when I was wrestling with my faith and trying to ignore God. Therefore, every time I came home, before I took off my shoes or shed my backpack, I would tromp across the one-room apartment and turn on the radio. This was pre-Spotify time. In retrospect, I know that at the heart of my need for banal chatter from the radio was to silence the most vulnerable question I had: was

I lovable? If my friends really knew me, would they love me? After turning from God, could He still love me? I thought that if I kept moving, I could outrun these questions, if I kept the volume up, I could drown out the doubts.

Frederick Buechner describes the longing within most of us: "What we need to know of course is not just that God exists, not just that beyond the steely brightness of stars, there is a cosmic intelligence of some kind that keeps the whole show going but that there is a God right here in the thick of our day to day lives who may not be writing messages about Himself in the stars but in one way or the other is trying to get messages through our blindness as we move around down here in the fragrant muck and misery and marvel of the world."[27]

Besides the incriminating thoughts of our own minds, it is important that we acknowledge the other accuser. One of the most effective lies Satan can breathe in your ear is that you are not worthy of receiving love. Regardless of your best efforts, regardless of what your loved ones tell you, regardless of God's display of love and goodness to you, he can spin it all. He can warp the truth and convince you that God's promises are all a cosmic joke.

This very lie is hidden in Satan's opening remark to Adam and Eve as he attempts to conquer the entire human race: "Did God really say, 'You must not eat from any tree in the garden'?" (Genesis 3:1b) Satan knew that this was not what God had said but beginning the interchange with a complete undermining of God's love and care for His children proves tragically effective. "The lie of the serpent in the Garden of

---

27 Buechner, Frederick. *Secrets in the Dark - a Life in Sermons*. New York, NY: Harpercollins Publishers Inc, 2007.

Courage to Receive Love

Eden was that God is an uncaring Father and so we should go it alone. Satan didn't dispute the existence of God nor His power. The lie was that God doesn't care. All the evidence was to the contrary. God had placed Adam and Eve in a place of security and plenty—and given them the fruit of every tree except one. His provision was complete. Yet humanity believed the lie that God is distant and uncaring. We still do. Still today, says Jesus, our problem is that we lack faith. We don't believe God cares. We think of Him as distant. We see this world as unfathered."[28] After all God's goodness, his relentless pursuit, and clear displays of his love for me, I can find myself agreeing with Satan.

While running to the Lord in prayer should be second nature when I am feeling attacked, the temptation is to implement my own methods. Work. Effort. Rules. These are the devices of human-created religion that will go to great and even bizarre lengths to try and make themselves acceptable to God.

Saul, before he became the apostle Paul, was an excellent example of a person who had all the best intentions to honor God and earn his favor. (I use the word favor here instead of love because I believe that Saul did not view God as one who loves but one who needs appeasing). And in the mind of Saul of Tarsus, he had reached the pinnacle. Here he describes his trajectory before Jesus turned his life upside down on the road to Damascus: "If anyone else thinks he has reason for confidence in the flesh, I have more: circumcised on the eighth day, of the people of Israel, of the tribe of Benjamin, a Hebrew of Hebrews; as to the law, a Pharisee; as to zeal, a

---

28 Chester, Tim. *Enjoying God: Experience the Power and Love of God in Everyday Life.* Purcellville, VA: The Good Book Company, 2018.

persecutor of the church; as to righteousness under the law, blameless." (Philippians 3:4-6)

Before his conversion Paul was excelling at his chosen religion. But all religions, taken to their extreme, teach us to hate, not love, as it causes us to measure everyone else by our own standards. We see this displayed as Saul of Tarsus stands in support of the stoning of Stephen, a faithful disciple and martyr of Jesus Christ. Everything Saul was participating in was, in his eyes, righteous behavior ("as to zeal, a persecutor of the church"). To Saul, Stephen was following a fraud, a defiler of Israel which would have appeared foolish at best and blasphemous at worst to a Pharisee. But not only did Saul witness Stephen's unwavering devotion, Saul had to have heard something else.

Moments before Stephen died at the hands of the religious righteous, he was given a gracious vision of Christ and he cried out, "Behold, I see the heavens opened, and the Son of Man standing at the right hand of God." (Acts 7:56) Years ago my pastor beautifully highlighted the fact that this is the only time in scripture where Jesus is described as *standing* at the right hand of God. Not sitting. Standing. As one stands when there is great emotion, and they want to communicate that they are supporting them as one wants to communicate love. This concept was too overwhelming for the Pharisees, and they silenced Stephen in this world forever. But before they did, he was able to say, "Lord, do not hold this sin against them." (Acts 7:60) The same words uttered by Jesus Christ as He died. Words that would turn the world on its head if we would just consider the boundless love of a forgiving God that they behold.

Courage to Receive Love

The book of Acts does not tell us what was happening in Saul's heart and mind after this dramatic scene but outwardly, it was clear that he was working fiercely to quell the doubts that may have been planted by Stephen's display of devotion to Christ. Saul's persecution of the church became thorough and terrifying. (Acts 8:3)

When we are using all our best human efforts to make our way to God, to keep Him satiated, and someone says that you can receive His love through no effort of your own, your initial response can be to recoil in disbelief. I would either become incensed with anger or feel like a sucker. When Saul finally encounters the living Christ in Acts 9, the range of emotions must have been wild. His name is changed to Paul, which means "small" or "humble" in Hebrew. Everything Saul, now Paul, previously knew had to be relearned through the lens of the gospel of Jesus Christ. This would have been humbling, indeed, but it also must have been exciting as he came to know, for the first time, a God of love. Subsequently, this God gave Paul the words to write some of the most incredible words on the topic of love.

The love of God for His people is the through line of the entire Bible. The repeated theme of the biblical narrative is one where the Savior of humanity, referred to as the bridegroom, is in unrelenting pursuit of His people, collectively the bride. It is the epic story of the pursuit of the bridegroom for a bride who feels unworthy and wants to keep running away. Sometimes the bride willfully spurns the bridegroom. Sometimes she behaves in ways that will prove to the bridegroom that He made a mistake. Sometimes the bride is just trying to hide because His gaze is just too much. The gospel, as told from Genesis to Revelation is a heartbreaking yet triumphant love story. But this stunning mind-melting passage of Ephesians 3:14-19 has become one of the loudest expressions of God's love for me:

> *"For this reason I bow my knees before the Father, from whom every family in heaven and on earth is named, that according to the riches of His glory He may grant you to be strengthened with power through His Spirit in your inner being, so that Christ may dwell in your hearts through faith—that you, being rooted and grounded in love, may have strength to comprehend with all the saints what is the breadth and length and height and depth, and to know the love of Christ that surpasses knowledge, that you may be filled with all the fullness of God."* (Ephesians 3:14-19)

It speaks of not just His love for us but his deep desire for us to know, feel, taste, and experience His love. He is inviting us to have more of Him in our inner being and wants to equip us for that glorious reality. He wants us to be deeply acquainted with His love. To breathe it in and live it out.

This passage in Ephesians is breathtaking. After redeeming and restoring Paul, God calls him to write these exquisite and mysterious words to the Ephesian church and to the church for all time. The irony is that after learning of the history of God's faithfulness to His people and Christ's radical display of love, this passage should have been self-explanatory, but, for me, it was not.

After a year of contemplating and studying this passage, I am still stunned by it; often either too proud or too ashamed to accept it. Too afraid to throw myself into the boundless love of God. But once again, I need to remind myself that, even in my fear of asking for the strength and power to comprehend

Courage to Receive Love

all that is available to me through the love of God, He doesn't want me to do that alone but desires that I follow Him in this. Increasing my understanding of God's love and how to develop the capacity to receive it is something that happens in close proximity to Him.

Believing and receiving the love of God is an act of loving worship. Taking God at His word when He declares His love over us is a way of honoring Him, but it often does not come easily. I have found that we can practice this in our human relationships. In the past several years, I have made a concerted and intentional effort to meditate on the ways my husband shows his love for me. Regardless of how unworthy or insecure I feel in these displays of love, I try to practice believing in them.

Sometimes it does feel like it's a 'fake it till you make it' kind of situation, but the more I choose this response to love, not only am I changed, but my husband is blessed as well. I have also extended this gracious response to others, and I have discovered that as I choose to take people at their word when they show their love for me, I have become a more loving person; less critical, less sarcastic, less guarded.

When I sit in Ashley's "I love you dearly" without dismissing it, downplaying it, or correcting it, I am, in a small way, increasing in my capacity to love and be loved, better equipping me to receive God's infinitely greater love.

There is an unfortunate message that creeps up in church sermons and Christian conversations from time to time that says we must 'be careful'. Be careful that you don't just focus on love, or you will end up abusing it, taking advantage of God or others in your life and won't take sin seriously. I believe the opposite is true. The more we study and internalize the love of God revealed in scripture; the reckless love of God, the pursuing love of God, the sacrificial love of God, the liberating love of God, the more we see that the sin we were once tempted by pales in comparison. Nancy Pearcey encourages us to create a robust Biblical worldview in her book, *Total Truth*. Instead of beginning our Christian story, as we are prone to do, with the fall of man in Genesis 3, she encourages us to start earlier with creation. Before the fall into sin, we were something else: image bearers of a perfect and holy God who created us to be the prize of His creation.

> "In the first six days of the Genesis narrative, God forms then fills the physical universe— the sky with the sun and moon, the sea with its swimming creatures, the earth with its land animals. Then the narrative pauses, as though to emphasize that the next step will be the culmination of all that has gone before. This is the only stage in the creative process when God announces His plan ahead of time, when the members of the Trinity consult with one another: Let Us make a creature in Our image, who will represent Us and carry on Our work on earth (see Genesis 1:26). Then God creates the first human couple."[29]

Pearcey goes on to explain that giving equal attention to Creation, The Fall, and Redemption allows us to have a balanced understanding of the gospel and our place within it. Understanding God's intentional design for His people helps us to comprehend the love He has for us and the dignity He wants us to walk in.

---
29 Pearcey, Nancy. *Total Truth: Liberating Christianity from Its Cultural Captivity*. Wheaton, IL: Crossway, 2008.

Courage to Receive Love

Spending time here also causes us to see how truly tragic The Fall really was and then how profound Redemption is. In response to the idea that says, 'be careful' when meditating on God's love for us, I am reminded of this quote from G.K. Chesterton's Orthodoxy: "The more I considered Christianity, the more I found that while it had established a rule and order, the chief aim of that order was to give room for good things to run wild."[30] God's love is a good thing that is meant to run wild. When confronted with the wild wave of God's love for us, run into it, crash into it, rejoice in it. Don't be afraid of it.

My hope is that those of us who know and follow the living Christ will have the courage to sit in silence, and acknowledge what is keeping us from receiving God's love; if it is sin, confess it; if there are lies, denounce them. Then, "Turn around and believe that the good news that we are loved is better than we ever dared hope, and that to believe in that good news, to live out of it and toward it, to be in love with that good news, is of all glad things in this world the gladdest thing of all."[31]

Have the courage to believe that you are dearly loved.

---

30   Chesterton, Gilbert K. *Orthodoxy*. Garden City, NY: Image Books, 1959.
31   Buechner, Frederick. *The Clown in the Belfry: Writings on Faith and Fiction*. New York, NY: HarperSanFrancisco, 1992.

Chapter Ten

Courage to Follow the Captain (or Courage to be Steadfast)

*"You can't test courage cautiously,
so I ran hard and waved my arms hard, happy."*
—Annie Dillard

Right in the thick of COVID-19, perhaps mid-2021, where there was a brief reprieve from staying within a very tight social bubble, we were invited to have dinner with another family. Vern and I were talking with the other couple when the conversation turned, as it did in those weird and wild times, to concerning, even scary, ways the government was making changes that were counter to our beliefs. We were leaning in and adopting grave tones when, out of nowhere, I blurted out, "What an exciting time to be alive!" If I had thought it through, the comment would have sounded patronizing and smug, but it was just a sudden, honest response that surprised even me. It was far more likely for me to chime in with my own anxiety-fraught opinions.

My friend stopped short and said, "Wow! I like that perspective." I found myself liking it as well and have been working hard ever since to see if I truly have permission to feel that way. In a doomsday culture surrounded by only bad news, it can feel like we are not allowed to have a more positive outlook. I wanted to know if I could be both informed as well as hopeful without appearing naively optimistic.

As I began to write a book on courage, I discovered some of the most life-giving and stimulating conversations as I informally polled friends, family, and fellow writers on their thoughts on Christian courage. Sometimes, however, I began to wonder if they assumed I was writing a very different book than what I had put forth. They seemed to be looking for a treatise on how to combat secular culture, and here I was rambling on about matters of the heart and mind.

While I agree that living as a Christian in a very post-Christian culture requires significant courage, more and more, what was coming at me from many directions sounded more like fear. Instead of summoning courage, it felt like the temptation for Christians, myself included, was to fight fear with fear. Isolating myself, engaging in fruitless arguments where I needed to be right, comparing notes on ways our society was becoming more anti-God.

As I began to question the increasing anxiety in and around me, I started looking for a sound and Biblical way out of the scary loop that was playing in my mind. "When we make a habit of letting fear decide, we find ourselves owned by a cruel and unrelenting master. We make rash decisions out of a panicked mindset. Our frenzy causes a further breach between us and God, which deepens our fears. This is the vicious cycle of want and need based in fear."[32] Surely there

---

32 Whittle, Lisa. *The Hard Good: Showing Up for God to Work in You When You Want to Shut Down*. Nashville, TN: W Publishing Group, an imprint of Thomas Nelson, 2021.

was a better way to view courage in light of living in this, often, God-hating culture.

Many of us can agree that the past few years have felt a bit like the wild west as we have encountered new territory with unique threats. My husband and I began having increasingly frequent conversations about how we should be responding as Christians while so many voices around us sounded panicked. Amid the chaos of a pandemic, a war, protests, and debates, my husband came into the kitchen one night and stated simply, "Sturdy. We need to be sturdy. As Christians we need to be calm and thoughtful and… sturdy." I stared wordlessly at him as I took a moment to absorb what he was saying. It was so simple but felt so refreshing after many months of complaining and fearmongering. I thought of the powerful and majestic coniferous trees that we are surrounded by in our part of the world. Sturdy, strong, and able to weather a storm. Ultimately, steadfast. We began, over the ensuing weeks and months, to remind each other to be sturdy and steadfast.

Unfortunately, this did not mean that we sailed fearlessly and confidently through the next few years. Ironically, from the moment I began to organize my thoughts and lay words down in this book about courage, we have known more moments of fear and doubt than ever. There was a moment near the beginning of the book-writing process where we were awaiting the bank's decision on a mortgage renewal. After months of unstable work for both of us, a renewed mortgage was not a guarantee, and the bank was taking an excruciatingly long time to decide.

I was standing on the steps off our deck while my husband distracted himself with yard work, and we updated each other on the status of the mortgage situation. Finally, having nothing to say, we stared at each other with frightened eyes, and my husband blurted out, "It's your fault! It's because you're writing a book on courage!"

"I know! I'm sorry!" And we both burst out laughing at the absurdity of it all. (It wasn't the last time I would feel like a fraud as I wrote a book on courage.) However, as we determined to remind each other of the target of our life, to know Christ, and the imperative to remain steadfast, we were able to pull each other back from the brink of panic again and again.

Steadfastness is synonymous with perseverance and can be used interchangeably in the Bible. It means to be resolutely firm and unwavering. In the context of our faith, it is to be firmly fixed on the gospel of Jesus Christ and not subject to change, to be firm in belief and determination, and to be loyal and faithful to the God who has called us. The word can conjure up images from many favorite battle movies where the heroes are facing an angry horde, and the only option is to fight when you really just want to run for your lives. Inevitably, as the courage of the "good guys" is flagging, the brave leader will yell out, "Stand your ground!"

That is the image of steadfastness that we are to have. But in the context of living in this, or any, cultural moment, it is essential to remember that the steadfastness that God desires to see developed is not necessarily, the outward swagger and bluster that some Christians are encouraging but something internally transformative: "Count it all joy, my brothers, when you meet trials of various kinds, for you know that the testing of your faith produces steadfastness. And let steadfastness have its full effect, that you may be perfect and complete, lacking in

Courage to Follow the Captain

nothing." (James 1:2-4) It was very helpful to discover that the word 'perfect' in this verse refers to wholeness. God wants us to be steadfast so that we will become whole, not fractured or out of joint, but whole and complete image bearers, ready and able to proclaim the gospel to a hurting world.

When I first heard the following quote by John Mark Comer, I wasn't sure it could really be true: "Most scholars would argue that Jesus was deliberately quiet and provocatively silent on the political issues of His day and that His silence was a greater statement than anything He could have ever said."[33] As I scoured the four gospels looking to prove Comer wrong, I couldn't. Without exception, the only people Jesus rebukes or openly displays anger toward are the religious self-righteous.

His heart is for His people, and His heartache is over their unwillingness to love Him more than the idols they are so prone to create. "O Jerusalem, Jerusalem, the city that kills the prophets and stones those who are sent to it! How often would I have gathered your children together as a hen gathers her brood under her wings, and you were not willing!" (Matthew 23:37) There is not one moment where Christ criticizes, laments, or pronounces judgment over the hostile culture He finds Himself in. We know from the standards of holiness put forth in the Bible that the ancient Roman culture would have been vile and offensive in countless ways to a holy God, but He is calling for the purity and holiness of His people, not the secular Roman society.

Furthermore, once Jesus does have disciples who have come to Him with contrition and true repentance, He doesn't

---

33 Comer, John Mark. 2021. "A Community of Peacemakers in a Culture of Political Polarization." Portland, Oregon, March 14, 2021.

charge them to police their culture through moral reform. In fact, He only has one job for them to accomplish: "And Jesus came and said to them, 'All authority in heaven and on earth has been given to me. Go therefore and make disciples of all nations, baptizing them in the name of the Father and of the Son and of the Holy Spirit, teaching them to observe all that I have commanded you. And behold, I am with you always, to the end of the age.'" (Matthew 28:18-20)

Again, at the beginning of Acts we read: "you will be my witnesses in Jerusalem and in all Judea and Samaria, and to the end of the earth." (Acts 1:8b) A quick read through of the entire book of Acts yielded the same epiphany as reading through the gospels; the focus for the disciples of Christ in a society that hated them, was to preach the gospel of Jesus Christ. Paul is arrested in Acts 21 by the Pharisees for bringing a gentile into the inner temple which was a violation of a Jewish law. Due to Paul's influence over the people, the Pharisees wanted him dead.

This begins a time of court trials and imprisonment that would last for at least two years and end with another two years of house arrest for Paul in Rome. While Paul defends himself before his accusers at various points, he understands that the main purpose of his arrest is to proclaim the gospel. After his first trial, where he describes his conversion story before a prominent audience, God encourages Paul that his arrest is being used for good: "The following night the Lord stood by him and said, 'Take courage, for as you have testified to the facts about me in Jerusalem, so you must testify also in Rome.'" (Acts 23:11)

The main concern is not defending his own personal rights and freedoms, nor is he standing up for Christian values. Paul

Courage to Follow the Captain

uses this unique opportunity to proclaim the "reason for the hope that he has" (1 Peter 3:15), and he is fulfilling the great commission by preaching the gospel. During his trial, Paul shows no sign of retreat or cowardice as he preaches directly and unflinchingly to his audience, but he also never mocks or demeans those in authority over him. Paul's response to King Agrippa shows the clarity and confidence he has in his reason for being on trial: "And Agrippa said to Paul, 'In a short time would you persuade me to be a Christian?' And Paul said, 'Whether short or long, I would to God that not only you but also all who hear me this day might become such as I am—except for these chains.'" (Acts 26:28-29)

Paul is clear that he would rather not be imprisoned but his main objective is that his hearers would come to know the saving power of the resurrected Messiah. After this last trial, he was sentenced to house arrest and, again, the scene does not portray dismal and defeated Christians hanging their head while Paul miserably bides his time and rails against the government: "He lived there two whole years at his own expense, and welcomed all who came to him, proclaiming the kingdom of God and teaching about the Lord Jesus Christ with all boldness and without hindrance." (Acts 28:30-31) Without hindrance. Those are the final two words of the Book of Acts, showing that the message and power of the gospel could not be contained.

It must be stated that taking opportunities such as the apostles took to share the gospel requires immense courage. While we are not living in ancient Rome, it is becoming increasingly evident that, as Christians, we are living in hostile territory. But I don't believe that the Biblical reference to have the courage to share the gospel is what we are considering much of the time. Courage is often mentioned regarding social or moral reform at a political level. There are knowing glances, exasperated sighs, and eye rolls toward many of the current ideologies or laws being passed.

Coincidentally, these reactions are common among non-Christians as well. Someone recently pointed out that if this is our only reaction to the culture then we are no different from those who do not know Christ. Essentially, we are missing the point and neglecting the mandate of the Great Commission. As Jon Tyson, pastor at Church of the City New York, reminds us, "We are not at war with the world. We are at war *for* the world."

In Russell Moore's encouraging book, *Courage to Stand*, he does an excellent job of reminding Christians where their focus should be. In a world that can often feel like it has gone mad, I find that I need to be continually redirected toward the truth of the gospel and the promises of God rather than becoming entrenched in every debate or engaging in every political struggle. It is a relief to remember that I am not obligated to fight every battle. "Speaking to the issues of the day or actively disagreeing with a societal norm that contradicts a foundational Biblical principle can be an act of courage. But it is just as important to realize that it may not necessarily be so and to weigh our words and actions well. Jesus often refused to engage in debates going on around Him."[34]

There have been issues that have caused me to engage on a more public scale to see change, such as joining fundraisers to fight human trafficking. However, in these times, I try to

---

34 Moore, Russell. *The Courage to Stand: Facing Your Fear Without Losing Your Soul.* Nashville, TN: B & H Publishing, 2020.

Courage to Follow the Captain

ask myself if my reputation for fighting for that particular cause has eclipsed my reputation as a Christ-follower or if I am causing other believers to feel like it is their obligation to join my fight. Again, Moore states, "No matter what people assume, there is no call for Christians to participate in every argument going on around them."[35]

A dangerous byproduct of that sense of duty and obligation toward fighting all the battles is a tendency for Christians to join forces with non-Christian culture warriors. While I understand the temptation to align oneself to the brave voices willing to risk being counterculture and unpopular, it is not leading us toward the goal that Christ called us to in the gospels. As Peter reminds us, "But you are a chosen race, a royal priesthood, a holy nation, a people for his own possession, that you may proclaim the excellencies of Him who called you out of darkness into his marvelous light." (1 Peter 2:9)

While there may be an opportunity for us to engage with the world on a political level and work with non-Christians in the process, they should not be our gurus. The work they are doing, no matter how closely aligned to our beliefs or values, should not be what gives us hope.

A friend of mine went to hear a prominent speaker who is known for his often wise and counterculture ideologies. She said that much of what he spoke about was intelligent, profound, and helpful. Yet what made her sad as a Christian was that in this arena filled with thousands of people coming for answers and maybe even hope, they could not be given the ultimate answer which is life in Christ. While gaining

---

35 Moore, Russell. *The Courage to Stand: Facing Your Fear Without Losing Your Soul.* Nashville, TN: B & H Publishing, 2020.

some wisdom and sound advice, they were still void of the transcendent life and peace that we can have through Jesus.

So, the question becomes, in these shaky times where the voices are loud and usually counter to everything we hear in a Sunday morning service, can we be joyful? Can we have hope? Can we walk with confidence and be courageous? Yes. A thousand times yes. And finally, after all that I have shared in this book, I come to my favorite story. In all fairness, it is a strange and somewhat confusing story. In Joshua chapter 5, we come to a short but powerful conversation between Joshua and the captain of the Lord's army:

> *"When Joshua was by Jericho, he lifted up his eyes and looked, and behold, a man was standing before him with his drawn sword in his hand. And Joshua went to him and said to him, 'Are you for us, or for our adversaries?' And he said, 'No; but I am the commander of the army of the* LORD*. Now I have come.' And Joshua fell on his face to the earth and worshiped and said to him, 'What does my lord say to his servant?' And the commander of the* LORD*'s army said to Joshua, 'Take off your sandals from your feet, for the place where you are standing is holy.' And Joshua did so."* (Joshua 5:13-15)

After Moses died, Joshua was charged to lead the Israelites into the promised land through formidable enemies. In his beautiful sermon on this passage of scripture, South African pastor John Rous says, "Throughout the book of Joshua, the primary thing that derails the Israelites from obedience is fear. To Joshua, throughout the book, fear equals rebellion."[36] Israel is on the cusp of battling with the mighty city of

---

36 Rous, Josh. 2023. "Courageous." Johannesburg, South Africa. 2023.

Courage to Follow the Captain

Jericho, and while Joshua and the other leaders must have been painstakingly pouring over battle plans and strategy, Joshua has this encounter with the terrifying stranger.

Bible scholars have determined that the commander of the Lord's army is a Christophany, a pre-incarnate appearance of Jesus. The fact that He is allowing Joshua to worship Him tells us that this is not an angel but must be deity.

The answer to Joshua's question, "Are you for us, or for our adversaries?" tells us that often we are asking the wrong questions. The question should not be "Are you on our side?" but "Are we on *your* side?" Essentially, the Lord is reminding Joshua that He is leading the battle and to follow His lead is the only way forward. The story belongs to God and our job is to follow. John Rous says, "What God wanted to do through the Israelites, which was to defeat Jericho, was not as important as what He wanted to do in them, which was to teach them obedience."[37]

What follows in Joshua 6 and the defeat of Jericho is an incredible reminder that the plans and purposes of God can be achieved in the strangest or surprising ways. Often having courage can mean walking forward in obedience when nothing makes sense or feels glamorous, trusting that God is doing the work. As we look to the work of Jesus on the cross, there is no greater example of God using something weak to upend all of creation to restore humanity.

I believe that in ending my book with the story of Joshua and the Captain of the Lord's Army, I am leaving us with a rallying cry and an anthem. Gradually, as I meditate on the many reasons we must live our lives with courage, I can really start to believe my words to my friend two years ago. What an

---

37 Rous, Josh. 2023. "Courageous." Johannesburg, South Africa. 2023.

exciting time to be alive! As believers in a sovereign God, we know that the fact that we are alive right now is not a mistake. He has ordained us to be here "for such a time as this" and has not left us alone. We have the Captain. He goes before us. He knows where he is going, and he has promised that none of his children will be lost along the way (Jude 1:1).

"Instead of asking you to toughen up, God asks you to look up. Look to the one who has already entered the valley to fight on your behalf. God didn't give us the story of David and Goliath, so we could live more courageously and take down Anxiety. He gave us this story so that in every daunting circumstance, we would see Jesus. If we had to fight anxiety by our willpower, then all hope would be lost."[38] The antidote to fear is not shame, denial, or avoidance. The path to courage is through fear with faith and obedience as we lean into our mighty God who loves us and has called us out of darkness and into his marvelous light.

---

[38] Palpant, Ben. *Letters From The Mountain*. Nashville, TN: Rabbit Room Press, 2021.

Appendix

Book Study Questions

I have had the pleasure and privilege of being part of a book club for years. The laughter, tears, wine, and occasional conversations about the book shaped my life in profound ways. When we did get around to actually talking about the book we were reading, I was always amazed at how much more I could get out of the book when we all put our heads together and I could listen to the perspectives, opinions, and insights of others. If it was a good night we would have rousing debates and one time my friend accidentally left with two different shoes!

If you have chosen this book for your book club selection, thank you! I have added some questions to perhaps get the discussions flowing. Definitely feel free to do your own thing though. It can be very helpful to look up the scripture references to make sure the context is correct or sit in some of the beautiful quotes from the writings of others I have included. Please know that I am always open to questions or comments that may arise from your reading of this book. Feel free to contact me: thesacredandtheabsurd@gmail.com. Blessings.

Introduction

1. Is courage a character trait that you have focused on in your life? Does it feel like a trait reserved for people living in other times or places?
2. When you hear the call to Christian courage what does that sound like to you? How does that impact how you view God and His perspective of you?

Chapter 1 - The Call to Courage

1. In navigating relationships with difficult people in your life, have you considered praying for courage?
2. Spend time meditating on all the ways God has shown Himself good and faithful to you , as He did to Abraham. When He is requiring courage from you can you remember His goodness to you?
3. Consider how responding to a call to courage is not a "blind" act of faith.

Chapter 2 - Courage to Wait in Grief

1. Have you ever faced a scary level of grief? If so, were you able to draw nearer to Jesus in that time: or did He feel farther?
2. Have you ever prayed a prayer that you felt confident that God would answer but didn't? How did that impact your relationship with Him?
3. Is there something you are waiting for right now? I would encourage you to have the courage to wait.

Book Study Questions

Consider the stories of Moses, Joseph, and so many more. Take courage and draw closer to the Lord.

Chapter 3 - Courage to Pray the Most Important Prayer

1. Can you tell the difference between the Holy Spirit's voice and your own thoughts? Most of us can't all the time. What do you do with the thoughts that seem to come out of "nowhere"?
2. Have you ever been convicted to stop praying for something? Read the parable of the persistent widow in Luke 18:1-8. Have there been prayers like this for you that the Lord has answered?
3. Why does it feel more scary to pray for things like God's love or His holiness than for our physical provisions? Can you relate to the Henri Nouwen quote about the child with their mother?

Chapter 4 - Courage to Lament

1. Is the concept of lament something that is familiar to you?
2. Have you found your church community to be a safe and honest place for lament? Why or why not?
3. How do you usually respond to another person's grief or lament? Consider Jesus' response to the grief of Martha and Mary.

Chapter 5 - Courage to Raise a Prodigal

1. If you are a parent, how much pressure have you felt, from yourself or others, to make sure your child appears "Christian" enough?
2. Have you noticed the emphasis of the warning of the Prodigal Son without the warning of the Rich Young Ruler in your experience?
3. What can you shift in your parenting to focus on leading your children to love the compelling person of Christ instead of, primarily, focusing on outward behavior?

Chapter 6 - Courage to Trust

1. When was there a time or circumstance where the thought of trusting Jesus was just too scary? Why did it seem easier to trust in human solutions or in yourself?
2. Can you testify to the deep and good work the Lord has done in you when you walked through deep waters with Him that you could not manage by yourself?
3. In times when you feel too afraid to trust Jesus, can I encourage you to draw nearer to Him and try to understand His character? Try Matthew 11:28-30.

Book Study Questions

Chapter 7 - Courage to Release Resentment

1. When I mention the word resentment, what visceral moments come to mind? You will likely not want to share these with others but if you still have a vivid memory, then it is probably an area of unforgiveness that needs to be addressed.
2. Have you considered learning about good, kind boundaries so that your relationships can be more healthy and less likely that resentments will form?
3. Can you believe that the Lord has more to give you in return for your resentments and unforgiveness? He has more goodness. More everything.

Chapter 8 - Courage to be Humble

1. When you think of the word "humble" what kind of person comes to mind? In your own life, why do you think it is a challenge to seek humility?
2. Have you been afraid that if you seek humility, you will become less unique and more of a Christian clone?
3. When you are tempted to not pursue humility, can you consider the humility of Christ? Particularly described in Philippians 2:1-11.

Chapter 9 - Courage to Receive Love

1. I have a friend who finds it very difficult to receive gifts. Can you relate? If so, why do you think that is?
2. Although we all want/need to be loved, we often either can't notice the love that others offer or we don't feel worthy of it. Why is that?
3. Ephesians 3 explains that God's love is so all-consuming that we need to be strengthened in order to receive it. Do you pray for that strengthening on a regular basis?

Chapter 10 - Courage to Follow the Captain

1. If you think of first century Christians in Ancient Rome, how are our circumstances alike/different?
2. If we consider that God is interested, above all things, in our conforming to the likeness of Jesus, where do you most need courage as a Christian?
3. Read the descriptions of Jesus in, both Joshua 5:13, and in Revelation 1:9-18. Can these passages remind you that you serve, both a meek and humble Saviour, as well as a Warrior Messiah who has control over all things?

Acknowledgments

A large endeavor such as writing a book cannot be done in isolation. I am deeply grateful for the community, training, and encouragement of the Called Creatives community. Furthermore, the opportunity they offered me through Called Creatives Publishing allowed me to see a long-time dream come to fruition. The patience of Steph Meyer Kingery and Sarah Farish was invaluable, as were the wisdom and direction of Lisa Whittle and Alli Worthington.

The encouragement of countless friends, family, and blog readers came at moments when I was ready to give up on this whole project. I am humbled by their words and prayers. One in particular went beyond what I could have imagined by reading, editing, and commenting on every single word of this book. Ashley Luciano has been a faithful champion and also had the courage to tell me when I had to "kill the darlings".

Ayal, Sophie, Max, and Abi: you have changed me from the inside out. You have caused me to know love, honesty, and a fierce courage that would fight for you all my days. Know Jesus, my darlings. Abi, you were also an amazing and faithful editor. Thank you.

Take Courage, Dear Heart

To my beloved, Vern, there is not one person who has believed in me more than you. I know that without you, this absolutely would not have happened. I also believe in you.

To the God of my life, you have pursued and loved me all my days. May I continue to have the courage to show up for the rest of the show, from now until eternity.

www.ingramcontent.com/pod-product-compliance
Lightning Source LLC
Chambersburg PA
CBHW020244010526
44107CB00002B/97